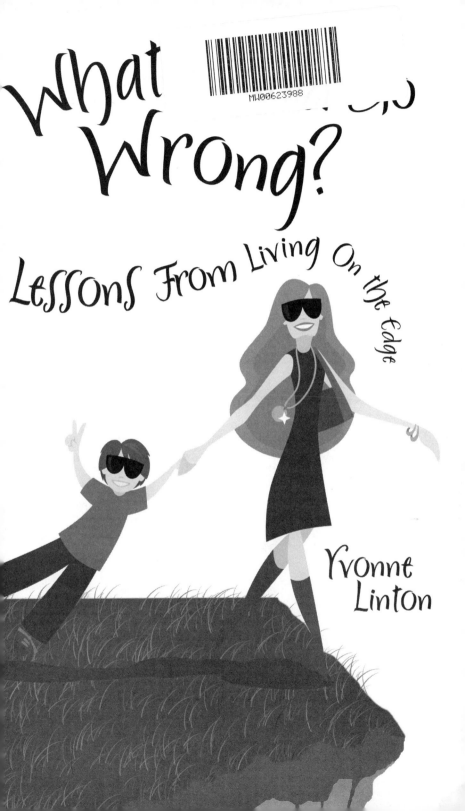

What ...
Wrong?

Lessons From Living On the Edge

Yvonne
Linton

What Could Go Wrong?

Lessons From Living On the Edge

By Yvonne Linton

Langdon Street Press

Langdon Street Press
212 3rd Avenue North, Suite 570
Minneapolis, MN 55401
612.455.2293
www.langdonstreetpress.com

ISBN - 978-1-934938-06-5
ISBN - 1-934938-06-8
LCCN - 2008936515

Book sales for North America and international:
Itasca Books, 3501 Highway 100 South, Suite 220
Minneapolis, MN 55416
Phone: 952.345.4488 (toll free 1.800.901.3480)
Fax: 952.920.0541; email to orders@itascabooks.com

Cover and Book Design by Patty Arnold, *Menagerie Design and Publishing*
Cartoons printed with permission of Mark Parisi

Illustrations by Pieter Plaisier
Printed in the United States of America

Contents

Acknowledgements

Thank you to the patient men in my life: Sam, Kyle, and Nico, who were forced to fend for themselves as I pored over my computer each day to complete this manuscript. I will make up for the late dinners, and the times I did not play with you.

I appreciate all my organized PTA pals and the PBC Moms' group who first inspired me to put this collection of misadventures and musings between two covers. A special mention must be given to all-weather friends like Rachel and Caryl who are brave enough to climb into a boat with me or loan me their vehicle.

I am grateful to my talented husband Sam and sister-in-law Lori Leinbach, and everyone who provided feedback on the early versions; to Pat Morris for mentoring me during the revision process (and knowing what I wanted to say even when I didn't); and to my editor Marianne Rogoff for prompting me to dig deeper and to reach the finish line. Many thanks to Margit Look Henry and Connie Anderson for proofing the final manuscript.

Kudos also to: Patty Arnold for creating a fun design; Julie Hachey and Wes Moore for dreaming up the cover image; Mark Parisi for providing the cartoon illustrations; and Jenni Wheeler for orchestrating the production process. You all deserve more praise than what I offer here.

Of course I also appreciate my occasional partner-in-crime, my twin sister. Hett, you talk me through every crisis in a way only true sisters can. My parents deserve praise as well, for being good sports about being portrayed in this book and for drawing several illustrations. You remind me to "Keep on the sunny side of life."

I give credit to my former publishing mentor, Nancy Kralowetz, who once said if I could sell myself like I could sell a book I would really go places. Thank you to all who offered to buy the first copy as I still have lots of places I want to go!

This project was a labor of love and I hope it will provide the healthy diversion and laughter we all need. May you all enjoy reading these tales as much I enjoyed writing them, even if they weren't always hilarious when they happened.

I thank God for each of you.

1 ◎ Prepare to Change the Plan

Proud to Be Average—Avoiding the Super Woman Syndrome

I was born three weeks early—an hour after my identical twin sister. It was the only time I had a womb of my own. This tendency for Hett and me to operate in our own time zones has followed us throughout life. We cannot blame our parents; they and the rest of our family are organized, punctual, and always prepared. Our sisters and brother maintained their rooms in a style praised by our Boy Scout Leader dad and Brownie Leader mom.

From a young age, Hett and I preferred a more casual approach to our surroundings. This we illustrated by yanking bars off the side of our cribs, curtains from their rods, and clothes from our drawers. I can imagine the conversations we had: "What shall we rip apart today? These bars are too confining. Let's go for a more open look." Signs of remodeling urges to come?

We did share the scholastic gene passed down from our father's father, a high school teacher. Our older sisters were models of this as well, and both have become teachers too. At the age of six we began poring over our *World Book Encyclopedia* set to prepare our first research reports. Afternoons often found us in the library in Roxboro, Quebec, where we absorbed all the facts we could find, from the camouflages of insects to the origin of babies. Then we raced home on our bikes to the smell of a casserole being pulled from the oven, escaping the chore of setting the table.

Teachers at nearby West Park Elementary praised our resourcefulness and thoroughness, but were less enthusiastic about the sixteen late slips our first year of school. Entrusted with walking to school from a young age, the lure of snow forts and prime snowball-making conditions proved too great a temptation to stay on task. Despite our love of the outdoors, the one task that needed little prodding was homework. Our mom often encouraged us to pursue more enjoyable tasks like cleaning our room, but we were more likely found propped on the floor with our notebooks, watching the latest Get Smart sitcom, or sneaking a book under the bed covers after lights-out.

Assuming the more time spent working the better the grade, we plunged into projects the minute they were assigned. Finding the work when we were done was a bigger challenge than completing it. Platitudes from family members such as "a place for everything and everything in its place" often fell on deaf ears but in time we managed to submit all work, skip a grade, and complete college by the age of twenty.

These early organizational habits proved pertinent later in life when I landed my first jobs in library science and textbook publishing. Initially I looked up to my efficient sales colleagues in awe but within a few years was promoted to territory manager, handling hundreds of accounts of my own. I have learned that we each have our own style and there are many recipes to success. Some will walk the straight and narrow while others forge a more creative route to get there.

Growing up with an identical twin was like having all your best strengths and worst traits reflected in a mirror. Eventually I became a mother and now see my single-minded focus reflected in my son Kyle. Then my second son Nico came along who reminds me of the secretary type that I am not. Sometimes we think our mirror is distorted; we want it to reflect another person. But we don't realize that person may look at us with the same wish!

Hett, now a hospice worker, once attended a workshop where the manager instructed each employee to complete a personality profile. The leader then asked, "Who would you most want to be like?"

Hett chose the woman next to her, whom she admired for her planning skills, and the same co-worker chose Hett, longing for more of her spontaneity.

My engineer husband Sam is a consummate planner, whereas I am more free-spirited, like my twin. My second career as a substitute teacher offers the perfect chance to combine both styles—each new classroom setting is an opportunity to follow a plan and at the same time "go with the flow." Flexibility is useful when little or no direction is provided. I have stepped in for teachers who were unable to put pen to paper as they were suddenly overcome by vertigo. I have entered classrooms that teachers had fled moments before when besieged by an unexpected stomach virus. Teacher notes have ranged from hastily scribbled scratches on an index card to elaborate seven-page instruction manuals that include how many crackers to dispense at recess to how many pages to read of the current novel. Elaborate discipline systems are suggested: dispensing cards or moving student names up a yardstick, color-coded by behavior type.

I always assumed that teachers had to remain orderly at all times, and that this trait was programmed into their DNA. And then I discovered classrooms where great learning was obviously taking place amid the cheerful clutter that prevailed. Projects dangled from ceilings or filled every inch of the walls. Instructor manuals were buried under piles of papers and locating supplies required a treasure hunt. As one well-loved teacher assured me —"My students know where everything is." I have gained inspiration in every type of classroom.

Parent Teacher Association (PTA) board meetings are also organizational laboratories. You cannot appreciate the amount of planning that goes into producing a major event unless you spearhead a key committee. PTA board members and parent volunteers often juggle part-time jobs along with family and school commitments. Some achieve all this masterfully as they build community spirit, fight for enrichment programs, host seasonal teacher luncheons, and coordinate fundraisers—often with toddlers in tow or baby in utero. Volunteer-of the-year selections are always a challenge since the bar is set so high.

When my oldest son, Kyle, first started elementary school I used to stare in wonder at these efficient moms. How did they serve tirelessly at school and still manage to wear matching socks and eye makeup? Noticing my deflated look one day, a staff member wrapped me in a hug and said, "We love you just the way you are!" From then on I decided to stop comparing myself to others.

To contribute to society we need not toil from dawn until dusk, the way I used to tackle schoolwork. This book is about thriving—not just surviving—in the kitchen of life. It is a guide for people who juggle many plates and are human enough to drop one occasionally. And it is for those who already know how to juggle and can learn new tricks from others. Hopefully it will remind us all to enjoy the beauty of our plates even when we break a few chips off the edges.

Lessons from Kindergarten—What Five-Year-Olds Taught Me about Life

There is no better way to test planning skills than with teaching a kindergarten class. Ever since I first dated my husband Sam, an engineer like my father, his mantra has been "Make a schedule" and "Have a system." Kindergarten teachers are masters at developing these. If you change any routine in kindergarten, you will receive immediate feedback.

Originally buoyed by the idea of a job that would enable me to work day and night, I pursued an Elementary Education major in college. While I had always longed to share my love of learning, I worried that I did not fit the profile of a typical teacher. I chose a textbook sales career instead—hoping teachers would be easier to control than students.

Expect the Unexpected

Twenty-five years after graduating from college, I found myself back in front of a classroom in Santa Clara, California, having been encouraged by my son Nico's third-grade teacher to obtain a substitute teaching credential. For my first assignment I arrived at school twenty minutes before the first bell. I strode purposefully to the front of the class, as kids streamed inside. The kids sat down proudly at their desks in their white and navy uniforms, sizing me up. The automated job line failed to mention that the class was a Spanish "bilingual" class, which explained the blank stares that greeted me as I issued the first instruction to assemble on the carpet. Each student had a pre-assigned square within a color group that corresponded to the color of the carpet row. My job was to ensure that they remained in the right place at the right time. The carpet is a wonderful place to practice listening skills and to share insights. For example, when discussing important upcoming events such as Halloween, one student raised her hand with enthusiasm to announce, "I was born on my birthday!"

Two students were then selected to highlight the current, past, and future days on the calendar. They correctly noted the number of days that had elapsed since the start of the school year, then progressed to the weather chart. It is often sunny in California, as evidenced by the fact that half the class sprinted to the door with the first few sprinkles of rain. All I said was: "See, it's raining outside." Kids always recognize a good opportunity for distraction. Once focus was restored, we moved to the important task of assigning reading groups.

Find the Right Partner

The teacher wanted the students to exchange partners. I suggested they trade seats with the person sitting next to them, like in musical chairs. This was met with an excited cry, "Ah, musical chairs" as all the students fled from the carpet, grabbed chairs, and hauled them to the back of the classroom. Not to miss an opportunity of having all children assembled nicely in one spot, I proceeded to play the game.

Kindergartners learn early on what I have discovered being a twin: any task is more fun with the right partner—whether it is bringing the attendance sheet to the office or being the designated paper-passer. Teachers learn early on which partner combinations to avoid.

You never know what conflicts await you in kindergarten. When I asked one group of students what countries on the globe their parents came from, one student erupted into tears thinking that another student had spoken ill of her native homeland of Nicaragua. After reassuring the child with a hug—I think that's still allowed in schools—I quickly set the globe aside to diffuse any more ethnic tensions. Children are very sensitive at this age. An errant tongue might easily be misconstrued. "He stuck his tongue out at me!" As a teacher I am part peacemaker, part counselor. "I'm sure Tiffany still likes you. She didn't really mean what she said about not wanting to be your friend *ever* again." These diplomacy skills are also useful for handling sibling rivalry at home.

Take Time to Play

Other useful avenues for diplomacy are playgrounds. During one of my first kindergarten assignments I thwarted a fistfight that nearly erupted over a popular recess game. Kids take free-choice time very seriously. Knowing they also take things literally, I carefully spelled out my instructions to a class of five-year-olds during indoor play time.

I reminded them to go to the activity chart on the wall and put their name in the corresponding pocket for their first free-choice slot. A scuffle broke out when several students double-stacked the names and tried to commandeer the playhouse. I quickly learned why there was a four-person limit for each center. To avoid future drama, I requested preferences in advance and inserted the cards myself, like a waiter taking orders.

A useful reminder in kindergarten is "Check yourself."

(This might be useful for some adults as well.) Despite my thoughtful intervention, one feisty girl made the choice of emptying a bin of Lego pieces on the floor, while another began using her crayons for target practice. This was hardly the picture of calm I had hoped to convey as parents arrived to pick up their little angels. I was glad this was not a classroom with a miniature camera eye mounted on the ceiling, like the one I taught in a few weeks later.

Keep it Simple, Clean as You Go

Kindergartners soon learn that *cleanup time* is usually followed by a more fun activity, like lunch or dismissal. It is good to keep plans simple near transition periods. Save complex art projects for earlier in the day. Part of the beauty of teaching kindergartners is that they are willing to clean up after themselves with the slightest of prompts. They know when they need help and are not afraid to ask for it, even if they all ask at once.

Kindergartners illustrate the importance of prep work, productivity, and play time. They demonstrate the value of a structure, a schedule, and a system. Beware of moving the usual last activity to earlier in the day: Students have been programmed like trail horses returning to the barn, and will start piling their chairs on top of their desks, thinking it's time to go home.

Decide What Matters Most

When teaching strategies do not unfold as imagined, it is best to have a back-up plan before all momentum is lost. Extra handouts are helpful for early finishers, as some will take two minutes on a task while other students take twenty. With the average attention span of ten minutes there are countless activities to pursue throughout the day.

Never lose sight of the students. Or the lesson plans. The main point is to minimize chaos and engage students in learning. Have fun in the process; remember to laugh.

Since many classrooms are supposed to be locked when not in use, an important item to remember is the key. You never know when the need for a spontaneous break outdoors might arise. Access to the key avoids having to stuff a tyke through the window to retrieve it or run to the principal's office for a spare.

These kindergarten lessons would have served me well earlier in life, when my tendency to live on the edge sometimes led to unnecessary dramas. I do not always learn the first time, but every day is a chance to start over. I have discovered that certain things in life cannot be anticipated despite the most fastidious planning. There can be danger in planning too much. Satisfaction is found in what you do in the unexpected situations in life, when you possess the strength and imagination to turn disaster into delight.

Formaldehyde Fred and Other Friends—Bizarre Business Travel Tales

If anyone had ever told me, "You will excel in sales" or "You will travel the country and get paid for it," I scarcely would have believed it. What could be better? This was not a career I set out to pursue, as I could painfully recall my elementary school fundraisers peddling orange chocolate apples door-to-door. (My son Kyle the negotiator fared better selling fresh-squeezed lemonade from our driveway.)

I began my professonal career in customer service, assisting seventy sales representatives for a leading college textbook publisher. I quickly discovered that I could do this job well too. This knowledge may have been influenced by my brownie troop days, where our motto was "We are the Pixies, helping others in their fixies." When a new territory opened up, I snatched the opportunity. I loved solving problems but loathed the paperwork that was involved before sales-tracking databases became commonplace. Whether driven by confidence to succeed or by fear of failure, I tripled my quota in my first year, reaching a company record of $1.6 million in revenue.

The lure of the open road helped launch me to the top of the awards podium. Or perhaps it was the rallying words from Olympic Gold medal sprinter, Evelyn Ashford, at my first sales meeting in 1988. "Visualize success," she told us as we all watched the clip of her award-winning, come-from-behind relay race. We all have the ability to come out in front, no matter how steep the odds.

Each fall I began preparing for success by pounding the phone and making countless cold calls for information about course sizes, decisions makers, and textbook changes for the coming semester. I enticed the decisions makers of my largest courses with glossy brochures until winter when the complimentary examination copies were printed. When my biggest sales prospects beckoned, I hopped on a plane in early spring to lure in the catch, competing against a host of local field representatives.

Like many people, I viewed business travel as glamorous. Then I became a sales rep and had the opportunity to debunk this myth. The only glimpse of local scenery was a passing blur out the car window. I experienced firsthand the realities that office-bound people rarely get to enjoy. They do not see the mad dash to catch flights, the midnight drive in the middle of nowhere on a near-empty fuel tank, oversexed customers, demented rental cars, and dead bodies....

Like overrated tourist traps, certain attractions I could have done without, but the characters I met along the way made the trips memorable. Take Fred and Wilma for instance. I was introduced to this couple prior to a client dinner and science workshop in Knoxville, Tennessee.

My plane had barely touched ground when one of my important customers greeted me at the airport and whisked me away. Our first stop was not her home, where I had been invited to spend the night, but a laboratory. Stumbling out into the chilly night, I followed the professor to the biology department of Carson Newman College.

"Come meet Fred and Wilma!" she exclaimed, guiding me through a set of double doors towards a long metallic table. Once I recovered from the overpowering odor of formaldehyde I crept closer to the dissected cadavers, marveling that intestines so eloquently portrayed in textbooks could be stuffed into an area the size of a lunchbox. Before me stood the evidence of too many cigarettes and Twinkies as the professor highlighted Fred's charcoal lungs and Wilma's yellow padded hips. Not wanting to spoil my appetite for dinner, I suggested we forego further details and continue on to our dinner engagement.

I vowed to forever skip sweets.

That lasted a week—life is too short.

In soliciting new business for textbooks, a certain amount of wining and dining is required, particularly when competing against field sales representatives who canvas the area with alluring incentives. Feeling generous on the company expense account, I asked a health committee chairperson where he preferred to dine. He slicked back his few remaining strings of greasy hair and happily replied, "Kentucky Fried Chicken!" As we stood before the baked beans, fried chicken, and buttered corn on the cob, he salivated through the gaps of his few remaining teeth and patted his protruding belly. I predicted this health sale was beyond hope but I appreciated the minimal dent on my entertainment budget.

Moving on to another health food capital of the world, my next stop was Alabama where I successfully upgraded all my anatomy and physiology professors to a new edition of our best-selling textbook. I looked forward to seeing one of my favorite biology instructors there; she had sent me sneak preview snapshots of the results of her stomach-stapling surgery, though I liked her just as much before.

My other hot prospects in Alabama were Introductory and Intermediate Algebra; on one campus I rolled $100,000 of business in one week. Having maintained a friendly phone presence, I was often greeted by professors streaming out of their offices to meet me. Those I was unable to meet were equally delighted with the famous California See's chocolate boxes I left behind.

Remedial math books were my biggest source of revenue, perhaps in sympathy for those who struggled with algebra. My Algebra and Trigonometry teacher had passed me on the condition that I never take another math course—probably never imagining I would be flown across the country to consult on a future series of math textbooks. My enthusiasm for one of our new algebra authors prompted one professor to return the hundreds of new editions that had been stocked in his bookstore and to order my product instead. (I paid for the shipping.) Introductory Economics was another subject that brought me much success in sales, despite my limited exposure to this course in college.

One night I was about to leave the campus of Grambling State University in Louisiana when I realized I forgot to work instructors of the two-hundred-student Macro Economics course. Management had considered our text a long shot for this department but this made me desire the sale all the more.

Pulling out my sales brochures and supplements from my book bag, I sought out the College of Business. Finding no one but a custodian, I quizzed him on which economics instructors were expected to arrive that evening. Like a teen on a blind date, I returned later to pace the halls and eye the clock. One by one the economics professors trickled in. I had probed the department chairman previously so I knew about each person's research interests and teaching styles, which snazzy test-generating software features to promote, and which supplements contained the latest hot topics. Not only did the department adopt our new economics text but they used it for several editions.

A subsequent trip to Kentucky to promote health books started out less than promising when my suitcase was sent on its way to Chicago. What would I wear on campus? There is nothing like searching for a Meijer's store at midnight in a jet-lagged stupor in sweatpants, only to be awakened at 3AM by a perky motel desk clerk, announcing, "Good news—your luggage just arrived."

Any challenge in life can be faced with the right attire? I failed to notice until halfway through a sales call the next morning that I sported two different black dress shoes, the one I had packed beforehand and the one I had purchased the night before.

Crawling along the freeway later that night amid driving sheets of rain, I was grateful for the pale glimmer of truckers' signal lights to guide me. As I approached the metropolis of Morehead, Kentucky, the center of the steering wheel popped out of its intended location, instantly jamming the spokes and restricting my ability to steer.

Luckily, a resourceful gas station attendant remedied the situation and pointed me in the direction of my next campus, where I had hoped for another health sale—a required course for eight hundred students a year. So determined was I to remain in the running for the committee's cut, that I had shipped a carton of supplements ahead of me via a cargo plane and a waiting taxi after just missing the Fed-Ex deadline.

When charming the committee in person failed to win me the tie-breaker vote, I brightened at the challenge of selling human sexuality texts in the Bible Belt. My largest enrollment for this course was at a community college that had been converted from a former K-Mart store. Imagine students lining up: "Blue Light Special on Sex Textbooks, Aisle 3!"

I sped across the Kentucky state line into West Virginia to drop off my rental car and catch my flight. I looped the airport a few times, like Clark Griswold caught in the traffic circle in *National Lampoon's European Vacation*. Managing to reach the gate with minutes to spare, I collapsed into my seat and arranged my possessions. Just when my heartbeat returned to normal, I discovered the remaining portion of the paper ticket had been accidentally removed on a prior flight. Somehow I talked myself onto the plane without it.

My seatmate proceeded to describe how his two previous bosses had suffered major coronaries at the airport. One had screamed at a ticket agent then crumpled to the floor; another became so irate talking on his cell phone that his nose began to bleed. While catching the bloody stream in a cup, he continued to yell. Both bosses died before ever boarding the plane.

On a trip to Louisiana in the early '90s, when my map betrayed me on the bayous of Louisiana, I resorted to knocking on doors. Fortunately a pair of friendly homeowners pointed the way to the nearest freeway onramp: "Left, right, left, another left, followed by a quick right, then veer left of the Y intersection and onto the blacktop."

I nodded brightly, pretending to follow the flurry of instructions. As the digital clock hit 10PM and the fuel gauge registered a quarter tank of gas remaining, I wondered if I had any hope of reaching New Orleans before hotel staff offered my room to someone else. To my relief the big yellow arches appeared on the horizon so I knew civilization was near. After tanking up in Baton Rouge I forged on to New Orleans, reaching my hotel just as a stream of fire engines pulled away from the front entrance.

By the time I parked the car and made my way to the registration desk, the smoke had cleared. Needing to wind down, I ventured cautiously into the heart of town, already in full swing for Mardi Gras. Apart from a few bead-slinging revelers and the strains of Zydeco music, the streets were happily calm.

Note: I was the person voted "Most Un-Rowdy" in our high school graduating class and was thereby forced to run around the campfire with a party hat singing "I will be rowdy!" (At least Sam and his pals hung the girls' toilet seats from the goalposts of their high school.)

On my next trip to the South I blitzed schools around Nashville, Tennessee. At the end of a long day I looked forward to treating myself to a rousing bluegrass concert and a room at the Grand Old Opry Hotel. Then I recalled my staggering new sales quota.

So I trucked 85 miles down Interstate 40 to catch an early start on a large community college computer introduction course. Based on the few decent lodgings available at the time, a key textbook decision maker managed to track me down.

When the phone rang I wondered who would be calling at such a late hour. His mind was computing more than software purchases and the high price of textbooks.

"Doing anything tonight?" he panted into the phone.

I wondered what my manager (and husband) would think of my customer rapport and how I would have the guts to meet the man in the morning. The swinging singles at the Grand Old Opry might have been a safer bet. I quickly hung up before his hard drive overheated.

Lying awake believing turning him down would cost me the sale and that I drove all this way for naught, I popped into Mr. Frisky's office after the first bell. After making a hasty exit I was rolling my luggage through the hallways, when a student mistook me for a stewardess on career day. I had to shrug and let it go: some sales are not worth flying for.

Another time I was attending a sales meeting when I was invited to the room of a high-level manager to discuss my upcoming sales presentation in Europe. He had just stepped from the shower when I arrived; thankfully he sported a bathrobe when he answered the door. This was not quite as awkward as biting into a cherry tomato at a dinner celebrating my sales awards—and spraying a trail of seeds onto the white shirt of the company president.

Amid my wrong turns and exploits I managed to earn the company hundreds of sales and remained a consistent top performer year after year. Management stopped trying to figure out my "system" after I earned the Rookie-of-the-Year honor and the Most Valuable Player nomination. Why mess with success?

It doesn't matter what obstacles we encounter on the road. What matters is how quickly we adjust our course and what we do when we arrive.

Beware of the Back Seat—Why It's Good to Have Clean Underwear

I have faced few obstacles in my life that could not be overcome. My first hurdle, at age one, was learning how to unscrew the metal braces adorning my pigeon-towed legs. In fourth grade I exploded in measles and chickenpox from the soles of my feet to the lids of my eyes and returned to school ahead of the rest of the class, after missing a month of school.

Then there was the bus incident in the seventh grade. The day had started out like any other first day back at school after a Thanksgiving holiday, with one minor crisis. I could find no clean underwear in my drawers, save for a bright yellow nylon bikini bottom. Since this was the middle of October in Quebec and the frost of winter was already coating the rooftops after a too-short summer, I pulled on a pair of tights over my plaid skirt school uniform and headed for the bus stop of my new school.

After plodding through the day, the final bell came as a welcome relief. I slipped past fellow classmates streaming out of class, to stake out a strategic spot on the curb in hopes of securing a coveted back seat on the bus. That was the plan. Everyone wanted the back row seat—perhaps due to the prime viewing area of the exhibitionist who posed daily under his partially opened garage door at the precise moment our bus passed by. Our Christian French immersion school had been incorporated the month before and contained only two grades so half the school population rode the bus. I resisted the temptation to chat with friends at their lockers about the latest teen trials, intent on my goal of reaching the curb first.

The bus driver pulled up the circular drive in front of our rented building and swung the passenger door open. Eyeing the jostling crowd forming behind me she pushed down on the gas pedal—instead of slipping gears into "Park" and asking students to form a line a safe distance from the door. Hemmed in from behind, I tumbled to the concrete. Feeling a lump beneath the wheel, the driver finally yanked up the parking brake and rushed to the back of the bus to investigate. Hearing the alarmed cries of fellow students, she peered under the side of the bus. Minutes crawled by. After repeating the Lord's name in French she ran back to her seat and desperately hit the gas. The wheel spun on my pinned leg as if stuck on a patch of ice. So she jammed the gear into reverse and drove over it again going backwards, as the tire ground through my pants and shredded my skin. I was finally extracted from the bus and saw that my tattered tights had been yanked down to reveal my half-staff yellow bikini briefs. The pain of the injury felt insignificant compared to the horror of having my privates exposed before the entire student population.

I did not win a seat at the back of the bus but instead earned a prime spot in the back of an ambulance. My question to the paramedic was, "How long will this inconvenience me for?" Two days later I hobbled back to class, having ditched my crutches after one day. The math teacher asked me why I did not have my homework done. Surely being run over by a bus was a better excuse than "the dog ate my homework!"

I may not have completed my algebra homework that day, but I did earn an Award of Excellence in gym class that year. When people hear how narrowly the bus driver missed shattering my kneecap, they tell me how "lucky" I am. Some people believe luck is our own doing and can be controlled by careful planning. Apart from discovering what a lucky person I am, I learned why we should keep up with the laundry in case of an accident and how we can survive setbacks with our dignity and limbs intact. (This incident may explain, in part, my fear of arriving early.)

It took a few years to forgive the driver for my crummy back seat ride but I remain thankful for the adventures my sturdy legs have carried me on. If one of my children or students ever roughhouses in line or complains of a booboo barely visible to the naked eye, I threaten to show them my scar from my run-in with the school bus.

Twin Travel: Double Trouble—Twin Mishaps around the World

My parents are descendents of French Huguenots who fled religious persecution in the seventeenth century and settled in Holland. They valued their Calvinist upbringing and Christian education, and wanted the same opportunities for their children. When Quebec's first Protestant Christian high school opened in 1975, starting with grades seven and eight, Hett and I were among the first to be enrolled. We had no idea that in two years our lives would never be the same.

Our father became increasingly disenchanted with the economic and political situation in the province of Quebec after the Parti Quebecois took office in 1976. French was declared the official public language in business and government and a referendum was called to decide if the province should separate from the rest of the country. Many predominately Anglo corporations moved their head offices elsewhere. Dad began to wonder if we would have to dash among three jobs a summer to pay for college as our sisters had. In 1977 he began hinting about returning to work in the oil refineries of Saudi Arabia. "Yeah right, Dad!" we replied.

Our father had fond memories of the place, having started his career, marriage, and family there—after wooing my mother from their native village in Holland. Once our older sisters started marrying and moving away—Peggy to Bangladesh and Marijke to Nova Scotia—the time felt right for Dad to pursue a new overseas opportunity. When our brother Mike relocated to Ontario for university, our family became spread over three continents and three provinces.

Saudis love children but were leery of the corrupting influences of Western teens; hence formal education was not permitted past the ninth grade. Brief visits into the Kingdom were allowed during the holidays. Shortly after turning fifteen Hett and I traveled with our parents to Arabia, knowing we would be flying back to Canada without them, to start the new school year.

At summer's end we stepped out of the airport terminal into the 120-degree weather and walked along the shimmering tarmac, waving to our parents one last time. As the plane roared off, our hearts were as bleak as the landscape beneath us; the only rivers in sight were the trails of tears spilling down our cheeks. But at least we had each other.

That was the premise as we went to live with our rather serious guardians (an older couple from church), and their adolescent son Bart back in Montreal. We may have traumatized Bart for life by sharing all that we had learned about human sexuality from the local library. Filling the bathroom sink with water to illustrate how a tampon worked likely put him over the edge. Over the next five years Hett and I completed high school, including one year of boarding school, and attended Calvin College in Grand Rapids, Michigan. All the while we ferried back and forth to Saudi Arabia during school breaks, completing nine trips in all.

Much of my thirst for travel may have been acquired from these jet-setting days with my twin. Given our distractible natures, I'm surprised that our parents trusted us to circumnavigate the globe alone from the age of fifteen. Perhaps this is why they booked so many six-hour layovers en route—they wanted to give us ample time to catch our connecting flights.

As a special treat, our brother Mike flew home with us on the return trip to Canada the Christmas of '78. A travel veteran at seventeen, he seemed the perfect companion to lead the way.

The stopover in Turkey was the first sign of what lay ahead. The Arab flight crew grew befuddled over the white carpet of snow lining the tarmac and temporarily froze in their seats. We eyed the cabin doors with great expectation while the Saudi passengers remained planted in their seats, staring blankly toward the cockpit and refusing to believe that we had landed in Istanbul. The stewards sprung into action but found no jetway to greet us, so they promptly sat back down. White-robed men and black-veiled women peered through the windows at icy drifts and then leapt up from their cramped confines, ignoring instructions from the crew to remain seated.

An animated debate ensued as we glanced nervously at our watches. Soon the jetway rolled over in slow motion to unload its charges off the plane. Other planes stood poised, waiting for connecting passengers. We watched the belly of our connecting KLM plane swallow other people's luggage from the gate, wanting to follow the suitcases on board.

Finally the doors of our plane burst open with a frigid blast of air. Trapped in the back of the plane next to the restroom, we tapped our fingers as passengers rummaged through endless contents in the overhead bins. First a trail of overstuffed duct-taped boxes spilled out; from deep under the seats other treasures emerged. Out came elaborate wooden hookah pipes, copper tea sets, and Gucci purses. To my astonishment a pair of slightly stunned, live chickens appeared next. They must have been lured to sleep by the contents of the bubbly pipes or the drone of the engine. Down the aisle the women in their black abayas and the men in their white thobes waddled, nearly collapsing under the weight of their industrial-size boom boxes. We could only watch helplessly as our connecting plane began to rev up its engines in preparation for take-off.

Hours later we landed in Holland and sprinted to the ticket counter. Naturally our connecting flight was halfway across the Atlantic by then, so the Saudi Airlines ground crew offered us a complimentary night's stay in the historic five-star Hotel Krasnapolsky, in old-town Amsterdam.

Only our brother Mike knew of this destination. Though he was just two years older than us, he had always felt it was his job to babysit and at this moment in our lives that meant protecting us from unnecessary trivia such as the location of the hotel. The three of us huddled on the sidewalk under the glare of neon lights, stomachs growling in protest. I pulled the zippers of my nylon sweat suit up to my neck, straining to see the city bus coming. Around me the locals commented on the record cold spell, evidenced by their woolen overcoats, scarves, and furry boots.

Half an hour later we stepped into the warmth of a bus, sagging with relief onto cushy seats. The rhythmic engine rumble and blasting heater quickly lulled us to sleep. When our stop was announced, Mike and I rubbed our eyes and descended onto the canal-lined streets.

As my senses snapped awake I turned to my brother and asked, "Where's Hett?"

Glancing around, my heart sank as I saw her head bobbing in the seat of the rapidly departing bus. We raced after the trail of exhaust fumes, banging on a side window until the bus coasted to a stop. Hett looked up with glazed eyes (wondering who had so rudely interrupted her midnight snooze), shoved her feet into her clogs and grabbed her suitcase.

My teeth chattered as I waited. Always thinking of someone else before herself, my twin offered me the jacket that she was wearing. Hungry and fully wired just in time to go to bed, the three of us headed straight to the hotel café, only to find the staff locking up for the night. We persuaded them to feed us, and an omelet never tasted better! Our unplanned layover in Amsterdam showed me that any setback can be salvaged with a kind gesture.

Another close call occurred in an airport in Paris. At eighteen years of age Hett and I were thrilled at the prospect of a whirlwind tour of Paris during our six-hour summer layover. We did the math and figured that a forty-minute Metro ride from the airport into the heart of the city would give us enough time to view the Eiffel Tower. Confident, we joined the masses of travelers being propelled up the plastic tube-like escalators towards space. The bubble-shaped terminals resembled matching spaceships and all looked remarkably alike. Flying cars had not been invented yet so we looked for the next best thing to bring us to our destination: the Metro.

We took pride in deciphering the schedules as we rode the escalator up until it spat us out in one of the largest parks in Paris, the *Parc du Champ de Mars*, which was much prettier than it sounds. We hurried past fields of flowers bursting in color, lovers strolling hand in hand and old men playing *pétanque*, the French version of bocce ball. The outing to view the Eiffel tower was almost as fun as the airport fire station tour we had been given by a troop of cute Dutch firemen on our previous layover. In Paris we acted as our own tour guides, though wisely chose to skip the long line to the top.

We accomplished our goal of returning to the terminal in time to catch our plane. To play it safe, we sprinted from the metro to our departure area, and immediately headed for our storage lockers. Pleased that Hett still had the key, I took it from her and inserted it into the numbered keyhole. It would not budge. Frantically I jammed the key in all the surrounding lockers, not remembering that we had stored our bags in the *Arrivals* terminal. I had not reached such a state of panic since the time I nearly lost my wrap-around skirt in the industrial-strength airport toilet.

And so began a love-hate relationship with airline travel; years later I recalled these fond memories the night Hett and I were trying to find her car in an airport parking garage.

Nightmare in Paris—When Good Jobs Go Bad

Many people endure their first jobs for the spending money they provide. Others search for something meaningful to do between semesters, careers, and dating partners. Either way, almost all of us acquire work memories along the way that we would sooner forget. We learn and grow from these experiences.

While in college Sam worked as a summer security guard protecting piecrusts. I always loved a man in uniform. Meanwhile, I landed a job with a local landscaper and Hett filed mirrors that failed to fit inside their plastic casings. The glass probably fared better than the grass, which never recovered from my stint with the weed trimmer—it resembled Sam's scalp the time that a barber buzzed it with clippers meant for neck hairs.

Midway through our sophomore year of Calvin College, Hett and I brainstormed about how to avoid the tedium of the previous summer of '81. We settled on a summer of finessing our French skills in Paris. (Our summer months had not thus far been money-making successes anyway.)

The whirlwind layover tour of Paris the year before did not do the city justice. We believed a European adventure would solve all our goals at once: get as far from Grand Rapids as we could, gain novel work experience, and earn some spending money. The decision now made, we fired off letters to various au pair agencies.

During the hectic week before finals, we each received a package from an au pair agency with letters from our prospective employers. Hett's letter stated that she would be caring for a couple with two children in a suburb of Paris. Hett managed to offend this family before even arriving, by failing to send them a "letter of introduction."

I eagerly scanned my letter for news of my host family. The elegant script stated that their primary residence was on Avenue Foch, a stone's throw from the famous *Arc de Triomphe* landmark. A majority of the summer was going to be spent at their villa on the coast. "How cool is that!" I boasted to Hett. I would be hobnobbing with Parisian elite on prime real estate next to the Mont St. Michel castle. Ever since our month-long trip to Holland in sixth grade I'd been enamored with castles. Buried in the letter was a brief mention of *deux petit-enfants*, which I interpreted as "two small children," paying little attention to the hyphen.

Careful not to commit the same cultural blunder of my twin, I consulted my French-English dictionary and crafted a letter to the family. We agreed that we would identify each other by my green school sweatshirt with bright yellow letters and that my host would wear a purple hat.

Two weeks later I stood once again in the galactic Charles de Gaulle airport when an old high school buddy, Sharon, spotted my sweatshirt and called out my name. She too had a summer in France planned and was thrilled to reconnect; we agreed that we would meet for lunch in Paris the following week. Sharon helped me search for the purple hat. Buried in the airport crowd we found a purple hat perched on the head of an elderly woman. A decrepit-looking sidekick huddled beside her. Peeking from under the rim of an oversized hat with puffed hair to match, the elder of the two spinsters strutted toward me. Together they resembled bosomed relics of the Renaissance era, bedecked in all their finery. They wanted to capture my attention so I would have no trouble spotting them in the terminal. This was indeed helpful as I was expecting a couple about seventy years younger! I glanced at my introduction letter. Then I noticed the hyphen. Amazing how a single hyphen between two words can change the meaning of a word from *small* children to *grand* children. Trying not to assume the worst, I put on a smile and introduced myself, and casually inquired about the whereabouts of the young, hip parents I had hoped for. They were gallivanting around the Grand Canyon.

Darting in their Barbie doll-sized car through dizzying traffic circles, moments later, I had scarce warning that I was about to enter one of the most prestigious addresses in Paris. With trepidation I entered the centuries-old building adorned with a pair of leering gargoyles. A concierge in uniform stood sadly by the front entrance, ignored by everyone but me (who could chat with a bedpost). The two sisters shuffled up several flights of stairs and introduced me to my *petite chambre* (more a windowless cell than a room). I toured my few feet of living space while I tried to filter out fumes of oil-based paint. As the thud of therapeutic shoes echoed down the hallway, I surveyed my surroundings and flicked on a light switch to shed light on my situation. Nothing happened. I tested all the outlets and tightened the lamp's dusty bulb with similar results. I wondered in what decade this room last produced electricity.

My "room" appeared to be an abandoned home repair project or a storage closet. A single bulb in the hallway cast an eerie shadow into the barracks-style decor. I barely had time to wrestle my overstuffed suitcase under the military-size cot when I was ordered to the main level for my first English teaching assignment. My charges were two brothers, ages seven and ten, who been deposited for the summer with their grandmother and great-aunt. Upon greeting the brothers in my most friendly-sounding French, they glared at me with all the enthusiasm of two teens reporting for summer school.

Early next morning a tinkling silver bell summoned me to breakfast. Never was I to hear my name uttered in the home. Henceforth, I was referred to as *la fille*, meaning "the girl." My meals were consumed in the galley kitchen alongside the other hired help. The ladies took their meals in the vaulted dining hall adorned with gold-framed oil paintings. A suited butler hovered at attention at the long narrow table with plush velour chairs, awaiting his next command.

On occasion, high-society friends joined them at the table, and together with their hosts made sport of poking fun at *la fille*. When they needed a refill, they tinkled the dreaded bell and out came another stuffed chicken on a china dish. Following lunches I was given the tasks of ironing the bed sheets and washing walls with ammonia-soaked sponges. My dream of charming children while absorbing French culture faded quickly as I became an object of scorn and slave labor.

For sanity, I polished off my one spy novel and emergency chocolate stash in two nights. I wondered how long I could ever survive a shipwreck if I could not muster the self-control to ration in a villa. Now, how to get through the remaining sixty days of summer?

I recalled my serendipitous encounter with my friend Sharon and hatched a plan to meet her for lunch the next day. How marvelous that God puts people unexpectedly in our path when we need them the most! I eagerly pulled out my Metro map and planned the route to our rendezvous.

Next morning we sat with our crème de menthes nibbling on baguettes and cheese in a Parisian café. As the sunlight streaked over our white-and-red checked tablecloth, I felt a ray of hope. What a blessing to reconnect; there's nothing like commiserating with a friend to gain perspective.

I surmised that if I were to avoid a summer sequestered with this scary family I would have to draft an escape plan; in a matter of days we were all supposed to ship off to the coastal villa that had sounded so exotic 5,000 miles and forty days ago.

Tasting freedom, I bade farewell to Sharon and headed straight to the Agency of International Au Pairs for a new assignment.

"Are you sure you are not just homesick?" the middle-aged employee asked me in a mock matronly voice.

I hardly knew where home was anymore; I had not lived at home since I was fifteen. I gathered up as many francs as I could feed into a pay phone slot, and divulged my plan to my older sister, Peggy, who had recently settled back in Canada after living in Bangladesh. With Peggy's endorsement I requested a new assignment and the agency offered me a nice, normal-looking couple with two sons. The mom was the woman's clothing buyer of the largest department store in Paris, *Printemps* (meaning "Spring"). How symbolic of a new start and a second chance!

I happily bid farewell to the jeering geriatrics. Upon my departure they presented me with a week's pay and the letters they had been withholding from my new boyfriend, Sam. Surprisingly, they had not been tampered with. I tore open the letter and scanned through the small print, eager to see how Sam liked the six-page collage I had sent him to commemorate our first few months together. (In high school I had once been accused of leading a classmate on and dropping him, much to his chagrin. So I proceeded more cautiously with male dates after that.) I was delighted to discover Sam's feelings were mutual.

Bolting from the scene I met my replacement, accompanied by her mother. I whispered a quick word of warning to her. Later I learned that she had followed her employers to the coast where she endured verbal assaults and shoes tossed at her, until her mom came to the rescue. She was relocated to a home for displaced au pairs until being placed with a new family. Perhaps that was my purpose in being in Paris—to warn her to escape as soon as she could.

The second family was kind to me and I enjoyed adventures all over France, including hiking in the Alps and playing volleyball with my topless hosts at their country home in Provence. (I was suddenly glad to have brought a bikini.)

One afternoon, I sat lounging with my hosts at poolside in Briançon, against the backdrop of the sun-speckled mountain peaks of the Southern Alps. Despite the beauty of our surroundings my mood turned gloomy, but I couldn't imagine why. Was I lovesick for Sam? Did I feel disconnected from my other half—my twin? Or was I just getting restless and ready for the summer to end?

Even crafting a love poem for Sam failed to boost my sagging spirits.

"Maybe something is going on with your twin?" my host inquired, sensing our close connection. "Why don't you call her?"

I discovered that Hett's au pair situation had deteriorated and she was, at that moment, on a plane bound for Canada. She had been dismissed by her family for failing to maintain the Mary Poppins persona they desired, and for accidentally feeding the family the prime steak intended for the pet dog. After Hett once waited with the family and pooch for an hour at a local restaurant, as fellow patrons and their bibbed canine companions lingered over tables, she was not sorry to leave this family. Rather than risk another disappointment she decided to fly home. She trusted her gut and never looked back.

Knowing when to keep going and when to scrap the journey for Plan B can be the best skill of all. Sometimes, pursuing new prospects requires a little prompting from friends....

2 ⋛ Know When You Need Help

Taming Male Tigers—Surviving Awkward Proposals

Sam, my first serious boyfriend, was the reserved type. I was the one who made the first move, with a little masterminding from my college buddies who knew of my questionable encounters with the opposite sex. My mom had offered ample warnings about men; I believed they could be tamed but my mother urged me to stay clear of the jungle altogether. Eventually I learned why it's important to listen to your mother!

My first run-in with testosterone was at the age of thirteen. *What could go wrong?* I was singing with my church's girls' club at a mission for seafarers in downtown Montreal, an outreach for international sailors. Feeling the call of nature, I trotted off in search of a restroom, down a hallway with many doors. A door swung open and a wannabe Romeo with a Harry Belafonte accent summoned me over. "Hey, gorgeous eyes," he crooned. "Want to come with me to my island?" Having no desire to dash off with a sailor I hurried back to my spot in the choir. Upon slipping into my seat, my voice raised a few octaves. Thank God our next concert was at a senior citizens home where the men were a little less feisty.

My second proposal came in Saudi Arabia, where my dad worked at an oil refinery. My parents and I were browsing through the old market "suq" of Jeddah. We followed the sheikh husbands and their black-robed wives along the cobblestone paths, absorbing wafts of incense and admiring 18K gold necklaces and bronze tea sets.

A man in a gold-trimmed robe stepped out of his shop, beckoning us over. "I give you great deal" is all it takes for my mom to cave.

We stepped inside the wall-to-wall carpeted shop. As we stooped to admire the intricate details of the handmade rugs spread out before us, the shop owner admired my blond hair and Caribbean-sea blue eyes (again with the eyes). My dad was fluent enough in Arabic to understand that the man was growing passionate about more than the features of the wool.

He asked my parents if I was "available."

To escape his piercing gaze my eyes darted to the floor, where he squatted on the carpet, haunches tucked beneath his white robe. There, between his legs dangled a penis as large as a prize zucchini from the county fair.

My parents, free from the distractions my line of view offered, steered the owner back to the sales negotiation and we left the shop with Persian rug in hand and my single status intact. The rug adorns the front entryway of my parents' home to this day.

The tables turned when I travelled through Egypt at age nineteen. My family and I were planning to visit ancient ruins along the Nile River. I could hardly wait to tour the Temple of Karnak, the Pyramids, and King Tut's tomb. Our suave Egyptian tour guide, Raul, handled all our traveling concerns, assuring my parents to trust that we were in capable hands.

The evening before our cruise up the Nile we dined on stuffed grape leaves, pitas, and hummus. As a special treat, Raul offered me and my brother and sister access to an opulent hotel on a nearby island. Like a secret agent he shook my brother and sister loose in the hallway and led me to an imposing set of ornately carved doors. Capitalizing on my sense of curiosity and love of history, he showed me where Anwar Sadat had recently stayed.

I peered eagerly beyond door number one to find a cavernous bed. Immediately I sensed trouble. Like an overzealous mattress salesman he encouraged me to sample it, but I had no interest in sharing a bed with anyone except my future husband. Before I could spin around and sprint from the room, this over-friendly Egyptian with whom my parents had entrusted me an hour before, pressed up close to lock his lips against mine. I responded with a jab of poor humor, "What are you doing, pushups or something?" His excuse was that he did not think I was a "loose" kind of women, but this was his way of finding out for sure. Right! I slipped past him, not having signed up for this part of the hotel tour. Later I discovered that he had tried the same "test" on my twin. Though Hett, always more passionate than her prudish twin, wondered what kind of kisser he really was. After that we were never so glad to see our brother.

Perhaps my mother was right—it *is* a jungle out there. I never told my mom this story about Raul, until now. Once I met my pussycat Sam the real adventures began.

Nutty about Love—Botched Attempts at Romance

During my late teens I could often be found hunched over a carrel in the seminary section of the Calvin College library. I was studying history and philosophy with plans to earn a teaching job or pursue a Master of Arts degree in public history.

One Friday night three of my friends decided to break me free. They snuck up on me in the library, slapped a blindfold around my face, and steered me outside. They stopped short of stuffing me in the trunk and directed me to the Fine Arts Center to catch the movie, *Elephant Man*. Several handsome male acquaintances were waiting for us there. Or was it that, after two hours with the disfigured protagonist of *Elephant Man*, any man looked like a prince?

After the movie my friends Sophia and Gerine invited us all to their dorm room to sip Earl Grey tea and mingle in cramped quarters. There were three male roommates and an equal number of girls. The best-looking of the bunch never took off his black and grey ski jacket the entire visit. Did he have an aversion to cold? Was he shy, or just ready to make a quick exit? I peered at his bearded, mustached faced for clues. This man used words sparingly; those he spoke were clever and witty. I wanted to learn more about this Carl character. Since I have trouble with names I made a mental note, so as not to forget it.

I soon learned that Carl was preparing to transfer to the University of Michigan in several months to complete his degree in Aerospace Engineering. I could tell he did not favor small talk but I found excuses to keep running into him on campus. I did not want to let this one get away. Each time we bumped into each other and I said "Hi Carl!" his eyes twinkled and the corner of his mouth turned up in a grin.

In high school I had attempted a few dates with a classmate who was too bashful to show affection. I would ask myself "Is he resting his arm on the back of the ski lift chair, or is he trying to make a move? Is that a heart in the huge swirl next to his Christmas card signature, or an attempt at calligraphy?" When my next love interest chose to break up due to my excessive study habits, only to change his mind, I declined. And regretted it. We went our separate ways and I learned that if you want something in life it's best just to go for it.

Now, not wanting to risk losing Carl too, I scanned the student directory to learn more facts about him—and discovered his name was Sam. I had been calling him by his roommate's name for two months and he was too kind to correct me. By then *Sam* was graduating in a few short weeks; I would have to pick up the pace since he hadn't made any moves yet. I learned he never dated a girlfriend before, so perhaps he needed a little prompting. Was he shy? Indecisive? Uninterested? I didn't care. He fit all my qualifications in a guy: funny, smart, and cute. I asked him out. Later he admitted that I met and exceeded his same three qualifications. He had considered asking me out first but could not decide on a restaurant or a movie; the closest flick showing was about a psychotic child killer and he did not want to scare me away. There was little danger of that.

My first date with Sam was an Easter Sunday service in April, 1982. The service ended with the Latin doxology *Dona Nobis Pacem*, a song where church members join hands with the person next to them. My friends suspected an ulterior motive on my part. Despite Sam's nerves keeping him awake the eve of our date, I clearly put him at ease. I do confess to remembering nothing from the service except the stroking of Sam's thumb against my palm.

Our next date ended with walking through the Burger King drive-thru at midnight. Somehow when we were together any outing was fun, even without a car, so I figured this must be love!

Sam moved to Ann Arbor in the fall and our long distance relationship began to sink in. What subtle ways could I inform him of my deepening feelings of affection without appearing too mushy? I had received an A on my *Communication and Intimacy in Marriage* paper but how did I measure up in real life? I turned to women's magazines for inspiration and concocted the brilliant idea of mailing Sam a coconut with the words "I'm nuts about you!" painted on it. Lacking white paint, I used White-Out. *What would Sam's reaction be?* I wondered.

I soon received his reply in the mail.

"I got the strangest package in the mail today. It was soggy and mushy and when you shook it, it gurgled. I opened it up with some reluctance, and there is was: a coconut. It was a touching Valentine's Day gift, especially since coconuts are not currently in season. Unfortunately it cracked and the 'milk' leaked out and it started to mold, but I have put it in a place of honor on my desk."

It was then I realized any man that would keep a soggy, moldy coconut on his desk must care as much for me as I did for him.

Soon writing letters daily, sharing a phone with five roommates, and standing in line for a payphone no longer satisfied our cravings for togetherness. Our first six months of courtship revolved around finding cheap holiday flights or bumming car rides to see each other. (This is how I further honed my travel planning skills.)

Sam began car shopping in earnest to facilitate future visits and found a spiffy burgundy MG convertible. Then he consulted his father, a former missionary, and his older brother Tom. Looking forward to top-down joy rides, I had to hide my disappointment when Sam drove up to my dorm one weekend in a battleship grey Toyota Corolla hatchback with 100,000 miles. This was only a slight improvement over the old Land Rover Sam used to ride in along the back roads of South Korea during his parents' missionary days.

Since I am a nature lover, I convinced Sam to take us on a spin through the woodsy back roads of Grand Rapids. We couldn't lower the top but we lowered the windows to breathe in the autumn aromas. I led us down roads that twisted and curved along majestic woodlands bursting with red-orange maple trees and yellow aspens. I spurred Sam to keep going and discover what new photographic opportunities awaited us. Each bend in the road brought another explosion of color until it dead-ended at—a garbage dump.

This was not true for our relationship; the experience brought my feelings to a new level as Sam smiled in his good-natured way, put the car in reverse and led us back along the same stretch of road.

On a later evening jaunt in the "new" car a policeman found us parked in an empty store lot. He shone his flashlight into our startled faces and asked for ID, prompting us to hastily peel our lips off each other. Upon relaying the encounter to my chaste mom, she replied in her Dutch accent "Vhat, not on the lips, I hope!"

Time spent together as a couple became even more sacred when Sam moved to Cambridge, Massachusetts, to pursue a Masters degree at MIT. Judging from the way it was becoming harder to focus on schoolwork we knew this must be the real deal and kept dreaming of our next encounter. Our halfway meeting point became my sister Marijke's home in Guelph, Ontario, where he popped the question to me one Thanksgiving Eve while pretending to say goodnight. For Sam to sacrifice a few minutes of sleep, it had to be serious.

Over breakfast I flashed my diamond-ringed hand at my sister and brother as I reached for the cereal. "Notice anything different about me?" I blurted, nearly falling off my chair in excitement.

Sam rang my parents in Arabia to request my hand in marriage; my brother Mike propped a photograph of our parents on the table so Sam could picture the folks to whom he was speaking. The plan was for them to meet each other the week of our wedding, scheduled for August 25, 1984 in Guelph, Ontario. My parents approved my good taste and Sam became the first non-Dutch spouse to enter into the family. He received high marks for being an engineer, a fourth-generation missionary kid, and a descendent of famed Declaration of Independence signer, John Witherspoon.

In anticipation of the long-awaited honeymoon night I scoped out a private room away from family and friends. Our former guardians and their son were staying in the hotel I had originally picked, so I avoided that one and settled on a motel room facing the river. Good thing we were truly in love as our first night of marriage was spent in a thin-walled room sandwiched between a team of baseball players. They cussed and trotted back and forth to their idling cars into the wee hours.

As we were at last drifting into a deep sleep, the front desk called at 5 AM to alert us to a burst pipe. "Do you want to stay another night?" the clerk asked.

We had enough sense to bail.

I could hardly wait to show Sam my old hangouts in Montreal and to tour Quebec City. Our plans were flexible as we were waiting to hear back from the American embassy in Toronto regarding my interview to gain permanent residency status. Being in possession of a Green Card would allow me to legally work in the U.S. and would save us from sneaking across the border in the trunk of a car or the back of a boat. The plan was to call my mom from a payphone each day and she would decline the charges if the interview had not been arranged. (Naturally we ended up talking at length every time as she probed for honeymoon details; if she had just let me hang up sooner, I would have gathered more to report for future calls.)

Once arriving in the 1600's era Old Town of Quebec City, we checked out the prices of the famed Chateau Frontenac and surrounding hotels. We devised an emergency back-up plan and soon learned that zipping the sleeping bags together in a borrowed pup tent does not make sleeping more romantic; it just means one partner will be covered with goose bumps as the zipper keeps sliding open.

I do not recall the moment—during the two nights of torrential rain—when the tent collapsed. The memory of waking in a tumble of soggy sleeping bags remains fresh. We disentangled and extracted ourselves from the mess and comforted ourselves with a delicious crêpe flambé brunch in a centuries-old restaurant before we made the daily call to Mom.

From there we moved farther up the Saint Laurence River and into the big leagues: a room with a quarter-fed vibrating bed and a TV with pay-per-view porn movies. Sam, ever the scholar, quipped, "We might learn something!"

Venturing ever farther into Francophone territory in Eastern Quebec, Sam dusted off his French language skills honed during his boarding school days in Korea. Feeling confident after successfully ordering "une am-burger and une large coke" at McDonalds, he tackled the challenge of reserving a motel room.

Upon hearing the remaining room options, he requested "*le room pour seize dollars* ($16)," thinking he was splurging on the room for *soixante* dollars ($60).

Previewing our Spartan sleeping quarters, he sighed in relief, "I'm glad I didn't take the cheaper room!"

Our closet-sized space boasted a light bulb dangling from the ceiling, see-through curtains, and the cozy décor of a monastery. I had brought along sexy black lingerie, a gift from my surprise bridal shower. Their inviting low-cut breast coverings were still held together by a clump of berries, which my twenty-three-year-old brother Mike had optimistically predicted would be chewed off in no time. The motel walls were too thin to fully put this premise to the test, so we waited until we reached our next lodging. This "motel," the only one available for miles, turned out to be two rented-out rooms in the upstairs of a family home. To reach our room we had to slip past the owners and their kids watching TV in the living room; we worried we would alarm them with our sounds of passion.

A decade later, in honor of our tenth anniversary, I had a pizzeria deliver a heart-shaped pizza to Sam while I was away on business. I tried to explain my amorous intentions over the phone to an employee who had not yet mastered English. I called to alert Sam that his favorite food was on the way in an attempt to stall his dinner hour. My man was hungry and succumbed to hunger pangs, resorting to his staple of ramen noodles.

When the lukewarm box finally appeared at the door, the lump of cheese and pepperoni inside bore little resemblance to a heart and Sam had to take my word for it. (Our little pizza debacle was still an improvement over my friend's anniversary gift of Chicago knives from her fiancé, which arrived the day after they had viewed the movie *Mr. and Mrs. Smith*, about an assassin couple hired to kill each other.)

We have long since disposed of the cracked coconut but we've kept the six-page collage I created commemorating our relationship, and the candle on which I had painted "You light up my life."

Though the words on the candle have long since faded, our feelings for each other have not.

After fifteen years of marriage, in an old-fashioned attempt to reignite a little romance, I e-mailed my beloved a waist-up shot of me wearing only a bra.

That night Sam casually mentioned, "We had network problems today and the systems administrator had to scroll through the e-mail accounts." He rolled his eyes and we both got a laugh over picturing the man trying to keep his attention on work after viewing such a hot shot. Thankfully I never sent a view from the waist down!

A few months later I persuaded Sam to attend a marriage retreat before checking the date and realizing that it was Super Bowl weekend. Sam was spared when I replied, "Never mind, we'll stick with our Super Bowl pizza and video routine. I'll forget about kneading it into the shape of a heart."

Hurrying with No Place to Go—Catching a Flight during a Freeway Closure

Who said getting there is half the fun anyway? Wouldn't that depend on where you stop along the way and who is in the seat next to you?

Several years ago I had the pleasure of a two-hour drive to the Detroit airport with my twin sister, following our niece's December wedding. Hett expected a routine jaunt, despite the ongoing construction along Interstate 94 and a winter squall advisory. Feeling confident about our departure progress, she took time to introduce me to all of her friends during the last hour of my whirlwind visit to Sarnia, Ontario. (She shares my compulsion to squeeze as much into an outing as she can.) The "Let's go to one more place; it will take five minutes" remark should have provided a clue.

The first half of the drive was uneventful and we happily chatted away. We congratulated each other on the excellent time we were making, surprised to see the signs for the airport so soon. Following the airplane icons to the terminal, we came across a low building with one propeller plane on the runway. We both blamed each other for the obvious error, then Hett quickly made a U-turn past rows of bungalows with barred doors and boarded windows. Careful to avoid broken bottles scattered on the road, she motored back to the freeway towards the metropolitan airport. It was then we observed a few cumulus clouds darkening the sky and the sounds of wind howling outside our window.

Soon, driving gusts of wind and sheets of rain were spraying against our window. We watched as water cascaded down the hillsides, causing small rivers to spill onto the freeway. Ahead two cars sat turned towards oncoming traffic, both victims of spin outs. Soon an accident was slowing cars in each direction as rubberneckers peered for a closer look.

As we drove along we counted ten accidents, complete with deployed airbags, ambulances, fire trucks, and speeding police cars. Just as we were marveling at how we seemed to be bypassing all this carnage, we crept to a standstill.

We caught snippets on the radio about "two semis colliding, a several-hour wait, and a freeway closure." Crawling along at five miles per hour with no place to exit, I felt the call of nature. Having no clue where we were, or how close the airport was, we fumbled around for our Michigan map to plot a new route. I called the airline to discover that the plane was leaving on time. Wouldn't you know it?

All the while in the car I felt an increasing urge to pee, perhaps due to all the torrential rain we were watching pelting down around us while we were stuck in transit. The auto state of Michigan offered few handy places to fill up a gas tank or empty a bladder.

Hett was determined to deliver me to the Northwest Terminal on the miniscule chance I could still catch my flight and refused to exit the freeway.

Was this perhaps retribution for every annoying thing I had ever done to her?

"Here is a leftover apple strudel container," Hett helpfully offered. I passed on the impromptu bedpan and continued to squirm in the seat.

When Hett finally conceded to escape the congested roadway, she had to careen across two lanes of traffic to reach a small gas station. Not a beam of light filtered into the windowless cave of a bathroom, but I managed to finish my business. Sighing with relief that all was well again, I noticed that not a scrap of toilet paper dangled from the holder. At least there *was* a toilet so I did not have to aim for a hole in the ground, even if I had to drip dry.

Returning to the car, I called the airline from my cell. "There is still space on the next flight," the agent assured me, after confirming that my original flight was now taxiing down the runway.

Hett and I were not overly concerned—until we approached the terminal. Flocks of birds swirled about menacingly, evoking memories of the Alfred Hitchcock classic. We hoped this wasn't an omen.

By this time Hett and I were cackling uncontrollably, ecstatic to have finally arrived. She dumped me on the curb to book myself the next flight, then disappeared in the direction of the short-term parking lot.

"Where did you park?" I asked my twin when she caught up with me at the Northwest ticket counter. Since I had time to wait before the next flight I offered to escort her back to the car. As the moving escalator led us to the six-floor parking structure, her eyes darted up and down the aisles in a panic.

Accustomed to attention lapses from a young age, we had become expert problem-solvers. We flagged down a parking attendant driving by on a golf cart and he was happy to help Hett, as by now I had to find my gate. This was a good thing, as there were 11,500 parking spaces in the garage.

As I waited to board I heard my name paged and received the message: "The car has been found!" This reminded me of the famed line from NASA mission control: "*The Eagle has landed!*" The amused operator wanted me to enjoy my flight without fretting about my twin for the next five hours.

Hett previously had little experience with multi-level parking garages. After our Detroit adventure we were both careful to note the correct letter, section number, *and floor* of our parking spot. Another lesson learned.

Meeting Your Match—Love Is in the Air and on the Internet

Remember the quote, "Life is what happens when you're busy making other plans?"

My high school friend Mark never planned to court his classmate Henriette (Hett), assuming that her bookish tendencies meant she was out of his league. A chance *Facebook* message from a mutual friend in the fall of 2007 led Mark to the "People You May Know" link. He clicked on Hett's profile photo (which had been helpfully downloaded by her teenage daughter) and noticed her maiden name, Plaisier, listed next to her name. This is the Dutch word for pleasure—the idea of seeing her again gave him pleasure indeed, for Mark had always fancied my sister.

The last time Hett and Mark had been in the same room together was at a twenty-year high school reunion in May, 2000. Mark worked as a negotiator for aboriginal land claims on Vancouver Island. He would never have predicted that within the next decade he would be negotiating a divorce and navigating the dating scene.

After a string of dead-end relationships, off-line and online, Mark did not want to take chances. First, he confirmed Hett's single status and then sent her a message from Victoria, British Columbia. For months he received no reply. He was about to abandon his efforts when he learned that Hett had never retrieved the message from her inbox.

offthemark.com

WHEN KRISTY CALLED HER BOYFRIEND, SHE USUALLY TALKED TO HIS MACHINE AND, WELL, ONE THING LED TO ANOTHER...

Mark devoted Christmas 2008 to writing to Hett (and to me) in a quest to ensure that she remained single until they could meet up again. He kept me in the loop, as he knew that if he were to court Hett we came as a package deal.

After months of lengthy e-mails and ear-numbing phone conversations, Mark and Hett developed a strong, clear sense of what they wanted in a life partner and began discussing marriage. There was just one glitch: they had seen each other only once in twenty-eight years.

Mark didn't want to propose long-distance so he traveled by land, sea and air to allow Hett to preview him in person. She wanted to see if he still sported a full head of hair, or if he'd developed three chins or a set of spare tires.

Hett knew Mark has a passion for punctuality, so she was determined to reach the Toronto airport on time. In the excitement of meeting him, she missed her exit and spent forty minutes circling back to the terminal. Nothing could deter Hett from this second chance at love.

Noting a pickup parked at the side of the road with its hood propped open, Hett felt a surge of sympathy for the stranded driver. But she was relieved the pungent smell in the air was not coming from *her* vehicle. As she approached the sliding doors of the arrival terminal, huge plumes of smoke began curling from under the hood of her car. With a sinking heart Hett realized the acrid odor she had detected earlier had not come from the pickup after all. The strain of rushing to the Air Canada terminal proved too much for her aging, secondhand Pontiac. With a final cough the car collapsed in the middle of the no-parking zone. Security personnel immediately pointed to the

"No Parking" sign. An important-looking airport official strode over to assess the situation.

"You cannot leave your vehicle in front of the airport, Ma'am."

"I need to tell my boyfriend I have arrived," she told him in her sweetest voice.

"What does he look like?" the official inquired politely.

Hett struggled to recall the details from his seven *Facebook* pictures. Lacking the technical aptitude to print them up, she had only her memory. Mark had thoughtfully provided vital statistics like height, chest and waist size, though she feared such details might encumber the identification process.

Salt and pepper hair or medium brown? she wondered. How current were his photos? How honest were they? Had he touched them up with Photoshop?

Hett's friends' foremost concern was, "Will there be chemistry?" The sparks flew alright. Mark could not help notice how unconcerned Hett appeared about the status of her smoking car; her eyes were only on him.

She's beautiful, and easy-going too, Mark thought.

He's cute! Yes, he'll do, Hett determined.

Once happily assured of the marriage potential, the next task was to find a tow truck. Sixty minutes later a harried driver squealed up next to the two new lovebirds.

Mark allowed Hett to set the pace but did not have to wait long for a kiss. Coming up for air, Hett noticed a car riding their bumper. "Boy, that person's really tailgating" she remarked, forgetting that it was her car trailing behind them.

When the driver asked if they were almost there Hett glanced up and realized they were miles from their intended exit, and heading for Detroit.

Having surpassed the 200-mile tow limit for her Canadian Automobile Association card, Hett figured that by summoning a local towing company to complete the trip, she could avoid paying the first driver hefty surcharges. She instructed him to pull over at the first exit.

Soon they saw the Welcome signs for a one-Stop-sign town that appeared to have sprouted in the middle of a cow pasture. The driver pulled up to a metal shed that served as an auto body shop, and found an employee who towed cars on the side. He suggested a fee of $20. By now a whole contingency was conspiring to get Hett and Mark home, from an airport security guard to two tow truck drivers doubling as chaperones. Hett and Mark finally arrived at her home in Sarnia, having driven through half of southwestern Ontario.

Mark aced his first stress test. Bonus points were awarded for maintaining a steady sense of humor and for protecting the car keys.

Next month it was Hett's turn to visit Mark. Not wanting to repeat the ailing car episode, Mark left his 1987 Toyota at home and rode the pedestrian ferry from Vancouver Island, intending to rent a car on the Washington side; this was allegedly more economical than taking his car into the U.S.

This aroused intense suspicion at the border. Convinced he was ferrying drugs, or worse, the customs agent grilled Mark endlessly for information.

"What is the purpose of your visit?" he barked.

"To see my fiancé for the third time in almost three decades" hardly seemed a plausible answer.

"Why is your girlfriend flying to Seattle and not Vancouver?" the agent asked.

"Because I couldn't resist a great deal on her plane ticket," Mark told him. (This was clearly a man after Hett's own thrifty heart.)

"Why did you rent a car?" the official continued in threatening fashion as he pulled on his rubber gloves. Mark imagined a full vehicle search and rectal exam.

Mercifully it did not come to that. The border agent reluctantly dismissed him an hour and a half later to rescue Hett from the Seattle-Tacoma airport.

My sister took it all in stride. Obstacles are so much easier to manage if we pick the right travel partner!

Honey, I Told You So—Why It's Good to Listen to Your Partner

My brother-in-law Mark finds it fascinating that Hett and I are so similar. Before they married, Sam provided a good preview for Mark of what life with Hett would be like. "Always have a book—preferably two—handy in the car as you will inevitably spend time waiting..." One of the other traits we share is lousy depth perception; we trip over the shortest curbs when we are together—sometimes simultaneously.

Our husbands are both planners, and accustomed to watching out for potential pitfalls. We appreciate our men for their sensibility but there are times we have treaded our own path, only to realize we should have listened to them.

My resistance to heed my spouse's advice started even before marriage, when Sam valiantly offered to teach me to drive a stick shift in the city of Boston. My previous driving exposure had been in the deserts of Saudi Arabia, where my parents had moved in the late '70s. Paved roads and street signs were a novelty there at the time. I tentatively grabbed the gearshift, like a scorching rack out of the oven, and eased the vehicle forward toward where I wanted it to go.

This was not where my beloved wanted it to go.

"Put it in first gear," he gently implored. "Don't forget the clutch," he added tactfully.

When he felt the car sputter and stall, his voice increased in decibel level.

"It *is* in first!" I insisted as the car lurched to a spot in the middle of the intersection while the light rapidly changed from yellow to red. The color nearly matched the shade of Sam's face as he stared in alarm at the oncoming rush of vehicles. Typically he is the picture of calm, but safety took precedence here. He thrust his hand over mine and yanked the gearshift into the real first gear while urging me to keep the clutch down.

Our next lesson was in the cemetery. He figured everyone there was already dead.

Sam still insists on being in the driver's seat, even long after we changed to an automatic. Perhaps this has something to do with a memorable snowdrift in New Hampshire back in 1985.

It was a perfect day for a winter outing to the nearest ski resort. The sky was cobalt blue and the snow sparkled in the noon-day sun. During a rare opportunity behind the wheel (early in our marriage), Sam gently suggested that I correct the wheel. My eyes remained glued to the small gap where I was attempting to parallel-park.

Sam suggested turning the wheel in the opposite direction, and I continued to maneuver the wheel my way.

He did not say "I told you so," which is what I love about him.

Sam is an accommodating sort. He chose to sit back, adjust his seat belt, and wait for impact.

It took me all of three seconds to launch us into a snow bank—better a bank than a tree.

Time has dimmed the memory of how long it took to dig us out; it remains a cold, fuzzy blur. However, I do remember a burly guy coming to our assistance and the sound of grunting and pushing as he and Sam disentangled us from a wall of ice. Picture Incredible Hulk meets Powerpuff Girl.

I had not received such a look of misery from Sam since I took him home for his first Canadian winter and his beard froze. This was the kind of cold where you wipe your nose and the glove freezes to the fence post or whatever it touches first. That's when he decided on graduate school at Stanford University.

He should have known—marrying a Canadian—that his exposure to the snow would not end so easily. Sam's antipathy for snow did not prevent me from dragging him into the mountains at the first opportunity once we moved to California.

On our first trip to the Sierras in the late '80s, we awoke to a flurry of snow swirling over our Suzuki Samurai convertible and its all-weather tires.

"Are you sure we don't need chains?" my husband, the realist, asked.

I, the hopeless optimist, replied "Four-wheel drive should be good enough."

As the snow continued to fall in sheets against our vehicle, I marveled at the sound of the tires spinning helplessly on ice and at how quickly our windshield had become a wall of white. Sam braved the elements clad in his signature jeans, construction boots, and suave suede jacket with faux fur collar. Huge flakes of snow plopped on his hair like giant bird droppings and dripped down his bare neck while he quickly crammed his fingers into his gloves. With a hint of a scowl towards the passenger seat, he pushed us out of the deep trench that my spinning tires had just created.

The next chilly episode in our marriage occurred during a bed-and-breakfast getaway to Bear Valley the winter before Kyle was born.

Along the way we stopped to visit a friend and Sam asked me for the map to plan the remainder of our route. (He had not yet acquired his most treasured partner: Maggie, our GPS unit.)

"I forgot to bring the map for that area but I know how to get there," I assured him, eager to reach the B&B on time for the free *hors-d'ouevres*.

"Let's buy a map at a gas station," Sam urged.

"I'll print up directions on MapQuest," our friend piped up, ignoring the furrow in Sam's brow.

MapQuest directions are a great help until you miss your first turn—which frequently happens within minutes of steering toward your destination. Important details like the distance between each major turn are easy for the attention-challenged navigator to miss. In this case, I also failed to note that the road had gradually veered towards the right, taking us up a different mountain altogether.

In most marriages, it is the man who resists asking for directions or looking at the map. In our case it's me. I hate interruptions when I am on a mission.

Isn't an occasional detour half the fun?

While I am correct a fair portion of the time, that time I clearly was not. Short of a military helicopter, there was no way to transport our vehicle to the other side of the mountain range where our charming B&B was nestled. My vision of a romantic getaway was fading almost as fast as the mercury was dropping. The moon beamed in the sky like a steady beacon, casting a lonely shadow in the middle of where we clearly did not want to be. At least we were better equipped than the ill-fated Donner party and did not have to resort to eating each other. Sam resisted the urge to chew me out and I ate my words about knowing the way.

I alerted the B&B. Our cocktail hour with wine and *hors d'oeuvres* would be cold cookies and milk at midnight. My little oversight would cost us over an hour of extra driving. I could almost taste the macadamia nuts and chocolate chips awaiting us. Graciously, the host upgraded us to a larger room when we finally arrived.

With this stroke of luck I was determined not to let anything ruin the rest of the weekend. Sam suggested we sign up for a snowboarding lesson the next day and I did not respond with my typical thrifty, "Let's just save our money; how hard can it be?"

I recalled my disastrous first skiing "lesson" from my twin's first boyfriend, and how much I had wanted to toss him off the cliff.

I smartly said to Sam, "What a great idea!" We would pay someone to watch us fall on our behinds every five minutes, and at least we would be shown how to do so gracefully.

Despite having a fellow snowboarding student slam into my knee with the force of a freight train, the lesson was a complete success. I know enough about the sport now to realize that I should pursue safer prospects like synchronized swimming.

Should I attempt to conquer the mountain again, I will be sure to have my safety-conscious spouse at my side. His responses to everything in life are "Have a margin for error" and "Put it under cold water!"

There are times, however, when even the widest buffer only gets us into more hot spots.

911 Bay Area Rescue—When the Husband Plays Hero

My face still warms at the memory of the stuck-in-the-muck-at-low-tide incident. Every woman loves a little action, but there are times when one wonders if inaction is the best course of all.

Having moved from the landlocked city of Dayton, Ohio where Sam worked between MIT and Stanford graduate degrees, we came to appreciate the water sports the San Francisco Bay area has to offer.

One late afternoon, about a decade into our marriage, I decided a quick jaunt on the Bay would be the perfect ending to a hectic day.

Sam was skeptical of the timing of our outing but, being the accommodating husband he is, loaded board and sails into the car and drove us to the rigging area.

Before rigging, I walked over to the shoreline and quizzed several returning windsurfers about the wind conditions.

"Awesome!" one replied, and the other nodded vigorously. That was all I needed to hear. The wind gusted at a steady twenty-five knots per-hour. With the perfect-size sail I would be neither overpowered nor underpowered. I imagined the magical sensation of riding the crest of the waves as the board propelled me over the water.

Where I saw opportunity, Sam saw potential problems.

"I wouldn't go out if I were you," he warned me.

"Oh, I'll be fine" I assured him, watching the distant sails carving jibes on the sun-sparkled water. "All I need to do is stay in the channel until I get to the deep water." I quickly donned my wetsuit and lifejacket, picked up my gear, and dropped it into the water.

As the sail flirted with the wind, I pulled the sail towards me and angled it back towards the end of the board to pick up speed. What I failed to detect was the speed at which I was drifting downwind, from the deep part of the channel into the shallow low tide of the bay. Cruising confidently along, I felt the unmistakable pull of my fin catching in the muck. The fin dug deeper and deeper until it refused to budge altogether. A breeze toyed with the sail, which flapped for a moment and then collapsed in a lifeless heap.

By now the muck had spread a trail of putrid brown slime halfway up my legs. This was not the thunder-thigh workout I had envisioned. I was ready to trade my wetsuit for a pair of Lycra shorts and a T-shirt.

To lighten my load I detached the sail from the board and began to lug one piece at a time towards shore. The foot of my mast has remained in the mud ever since, providing a haven for the local marine life.

As I schlepped along with legs of lead and beads of sweat forming salty rivers down my brow, I speculated about what Sam was doing on shore.

"Why isn't he doing anything to help?" I muttered, followed quickly by, "What could he possibly do to help me out here?"

I had launched myself into this predicament; now I had to dream up a plan to dig myself out. (Little did I know that Sam had responded to my dilemma by calling 911.)

Looking up, I noticed a fire truck poised for action in the parking lot.

Someone else must be in trouble, I guessed. *Maybe if I get desperate enough, they can rescue me as well.*

I continued lugging my equipment along through the quicksand muck. The bay slurped and bubbled beneath me with each laborious step. By this time the sun cast an orange glow in the sky. Most of the sailors were no doubt breaking into six-packs of beer and burritos by now. Then it dawned on me to furrow sideways towards the deeper sliver of the channel, instead of trudging in a hopeless diagonal towards the dock.

It was then that I heard a male voice beckon from the megaphone.

"Windsurfer out in the water: If you need help, RAISE YOUR ARMS!"

I had heard about the foolhardy exploits of fellow adventurers and the strapping bills that ensued. So I kept my arms firmly glued to my sides.

A row of figures lined the water's edge with suspicious round lenses at their eyes, pointed in my direction. I could imagine the entertaining view coming into focus through the other end of their binoculars.

At last I came within fifty yards of the dock.

Again, the voice bellowed over the megaphone. A sweating fireman stood on the dock with a life ring in his other hand.

Did he really expect to haul me ashore?

The last remaining rescue vehicles had departed by the time I finally emerged. Sam claimed that seven trucks stood poised at one point, but I prayed that that was a gross exaggeration. It must have been a slow day at the local firehouses.

Did I mention the inflatable raft and hook and ladder? I never had anyone walk on water for me before, so I was sorry to have missed that.

I cannot envision how many ladders it would have taken to reach me, or how the boat would have scooted over the sludge. I wondered what page of the emergency training manual this fell under.

I avoided that sailing spot for several months. Imagine my horror when a fellow windsurfer approached me there later on in my career, saying, "Weren't you the one who...?"

I am not sure how she recognized me since my face no longer matched the color of my red helmet.

Sometimes life leaves us wanting to throw up our arms in surrender. I was reminded that there is always a way out of the channel!

Later I read in the paper that the town is exploring a $5 launch fee for that site—they are probably still trying to pay off the rescue bill.

Camping for Dummies—Tips for the Outdoor-Impaired

There are few experiences that make me appreciate domesticity more than spending extended time in nature.

My exposure started at the age of two when my twin and I used to swing on our play set, scale trees, and shake leaves into the neighbors' swimming pool. This love affair with nature was tested by long camping trips with four siblings, a dog, and three weeks of supplies stuffed into the back of a station wagon. Along the way I have learned a few things to make camping more comfortable.

Lesson 1: Check Your Equipment

Even if you forget everything else, do not forget the flashlight to the potty on a cloudy night or you will have to holler for help to find your way back. Check beforehand that the batteries actually work since they undoubtedly drained long beforehand. Pump up the air mattress the night before to check for the slow leaks that leave you sucking dirt by morning.

There are those who truly camp and those who sleep in a tent. These are not the same types. The first group arrives with carefully packed coolers and a cupboard full of supplies. Breakfast is an all-morning affair with pancakes, eggs, and toast over the kerosene stove. For the rest of us it might be store-bought muffins from the 7-11 we stopped at on the way up; when we return from three hours of sight-seeing, they are still washing their breakfast dishes.

Camping in pairs is recommended. Then you can borrow from neighbors all the things forgotten from home and eat their tasty leftovers. The neighbors are usually the ones who make the reservations two years in advance. In case of rain, the prepared ones have elaborate plastic structures strung from strategically placed posts, while the rest of us huddle under a tree wearing recycled garbage bags. Garbage bags and tarps also double up nicely as sleds should you find unexpected summer snow. Like the time Sam and I discovered a fifteen-foot layer of snow lining the road at Mount Lassen, California one hot summer day.

The most important lesson in camping is to admit when you are out of your league. Before we had kids my twin and I set out to camp in the famed Yosemite National Park, where people pay hundreds of dollars for a prime spot. Having waited until the eve of our departure to test out the tent, we forced ourselves to remain awake through Sam's methodical tent-pitching demonstration. It came with a list of instructions that rivaled his Ph.D. dissertation. As he deftly whipped poles in every direction, our eyelids drooped farther and farther. Perhaps he should have offered an entertaining pop quiz with M&M's as prizes, the way he does for his Sunday School kindergarten class.

Hett had decided it would easier not to deal with the hassles of a campfire while we were camping. While I was at work she made herself useful. Accustomed to cooking for large groups of summer campers, she had prepared enough food to feed a platoon.

"I just wanted to help," she said in defense, when I arrived home to a mountain of potato and macaroni salad spilling over my countertop. After pulling her away to pack, I finally succeeded in pushing her out the door so we could start the four-hour drive.

We crunched up the gravel entry to our camp spot at 11PM, when even the moon was already asleep. We grumbled and stumbled about under the glow of our headlights, much to the delight of dozing campers. Between their interrupted snores, we crammed tent poles into the ground and coaxed a heap of walls and windows to rise from the rock hard dirt. The fact that the poles crossed in front of the entrance should have provided a clue that we needed help. Upon making a minor adjustment, we watched the tent completely collapse. Try as we might, we could not transform this chaotic pile of nylon and metal into a recognizable structure. I was beginning to understand why campers around us hadn't bothered with tents and slept under the stars. Hett attempted to sleep in it anyway while I retreated to the car. By this time we were no longer on speaking terms.

In the morning, we accosted a passing camp ranger who helped us erect our fragile domicile. The fact that he studied other tents for guidance only slightly alleviated our humiliation.

For the next tent purchase, I vowed to stay away from the ones with standing room for twelve, and go for the pop-up igloo-shaped style that explodes out of the bag. I will even read the instructions first or remain alert for all of Sam's demonstration.

Lesson 2: Choose Your Spot Wisely

Some campgrounds are first-come, first-serve. That works fine for families who leave at the crack of dawn. Families who leave at dusk end up with the spot next to the latrine. You never know who might sleepwalk into your tent in the night or what people might be doing in the bathroom. And you never know what exactly you are setting your tent on when assembling it in the dark.

On one trip, satisfied that we had avoided pitching our tent on any patches of poison oak as our friends once did, we settled down for the night. Tuning out the sounds of the desert, we could not help but notice the odor of dead fish in the air. Since we were hundreds of miles from the nearest beach, we wondered what our predecessors had consumed for dinner. Dismantling the tent in the morning, we found the flattened remains of fish bones and an anthill metropolis. The ants never knew what hit them.

It is also good to inquire in advance if the weekend you select coincides with the Annual Mosquito Convention, particularly when camping in Canada. Find a spot with a good lock box. If other campers do not threaten to spoil your family bonding experience, it will be the animals. Should you fail to stash away your food, a raccoon will tell all his friends and relatives within a hundred miles and you will be surrounded by intruders in the middle of the night.

Lesson 3: Find a Campground with a Host

The only thing worse than sharing your campground with the local wildlife, is sharing your site with party animals. There is nothing like the all-night sounds of beer-guzzling teens to make you pine for a motel. Worse yet are the adults who still act like teenagers. With camping you never know who your neighbors will be each night, but at least a camp host can deter an *Animal House* repeat.

Sam says there are two kinds of campers: those who stay up late and make a lot of noise and those who wake up early and make a lot of noise. One time in Bishop, California, I recruited him to investigate the whining howls outside our tent. In a sleepy stupor, I told him to admonish the voices to quiet down. Sam stepped out into the starlit night to be serenaded by a group of coyotes.

Lesson 4: Watch Who You Park Next To

For some people camping is a one-night stand; for others it's a long-term romance.

On one particularly rigorous road, we rambled through ruts and trenches, eagerly awaiting the rugged beauty that would envelop us in the morning. As the rays of sun lit up our campsite, we staggered out of our tent and discovered a circle of RVs around us.

How did they plow all the way up here and why did we not notice the hum of generators earlier? Around one RV stood strings of lights and pink flamingos to greet passersby. (In case fellow campers did not encounter any real animals.) These same people had their nameplate posted out front. They have brought everything from home, including the mailbox. We wondered if they had their own zip code.

Next to the towed jeep is a garage full of garden chairs parked inside the portable gazebo. Of course, now you know where to go when it starts raining and you have forgotten your garbage bag ponchos.

Lesson 5: Forget about Staying Clean

If you are an incorrigible "clean freak," forget about camping altogether. It's far too cumbersome to keep a dirt patch mopped. The same goes for baths and dishes; you might as well resort to wiping down with a Handi Wipe, washing the dishes in cold water, and rinsing your hair with the last remaining quarter for the pay shower. I have a friend who brings bleach along with her camping supplies because she finds nature so messy.

That's half the fun! Abandon the idea of smelling fresh on a camping trip.

Lesson 6: Find the Nearest Motel

The better approach may be to find a nearby motel and visit friends who are camping. This way you can still have that campfire experience and revisit your inner child.

However you choose to pull it off, spending time outdoors with friends and family may have you begging for s'mores. First we'll do dinner. Just be ready for Spam and spaghetti in a can.

The Gift That Lasts a Lifetime—Opening Our Hearts to Adoption

I could hardly wait to share my love of nature with children. Before taking the parenting plunge Sam and I made one last couples-only camping trip in the Cascade Mountains of Oregon, with our longtime friends Greg and Darla.

The eve of our departure I lay under our open tent flap peering at the ink-black sky and made my wish upon a million stars. Then Sam and I drove home, dropped a package in the mail and waited.

Nothing pains me more than waiting. That must be why it was taking so long for me to become a mother—I needed more practice in this fine art. I needlessly shift lanes to be closer to the front of the intersection, only to be passed at the next light. (My experiences with checkout lines prove equally ineffective. I now stifle the urge to stroll over to neighboring displays after nearly getting whacked in the head once by a senior with an oversized handbag. She exclaimed to her friend in horror, "Weren't we here first? Did she cut?!")

Statistics state that we spend nearly one-third of our lives waiting for something to happen. No matter how obscure the hour, we can count on an occasional stall. One minute we are speeding through the fast lane, and suddenly we are forced to a halt. Or a foggy drizzle turns into a downpour, then abruptly the clouds drift away and the sun pokes through.

The road to parenthood seemed smooth at first. Within a month of "trying" we hit the jackpot. Everything was going according to plan; our baby was due to arrive shortly after Sam was to finish his Ph.D. in Aerospace Engineering from Stanford. He already had a job lined up at NASA Ames Research Center. I had just received a promotion at my publishing firm. Life was good.

The night of my office Christmas party I started spotting and cramping. The gynecologist instructed me to come for an ultrasound with a full bladder. Being an overachiever I drank two bottles of water. It's hard to know what was worse, the probing of the ultrasound wand or the wait for the results. The Doppler device and ultrasound should have detected a heartbeat since I was three months along. There was none.

The doctor tossed the grainy image of our kidney-sized baby into the trash, saying, "There's nothing to see here. It's a nonviable pregnancy." What was that supposed to mean? I didn't even know how to grieve. I searched his face for a reaction, stunned that my doctor would drop this bombshell so glibly. "You may have seen this many times but this is the first time for me," I replied. He suggested trying again in three months.

Months of passion failed to produce a repeat pregnancy. Sam and I turned to fertility experts for help. Two more Christmas seasons passed, and countless injections of fertility drugs failed. Just before Easter 1994, I watched with trembling fingers as the stick changed color.

"It looks kind of blue," a cautious Sam agreed.

"I cannot be kind of pregnant!" I told Sam as I headed for the infertility clinic to confirm my findings.

When I later called the clinic for results, an unsympathetic receptionist told me, "There are lots of equally important people ahead of you."

I remained planted by my phone until 5PM to hear the news about whether I was expecting again. Dare I hope we would finally have a baby?

An hour later, I started to miscarry. I had prayed that if it were to happen again, that it happen early on. So this was an answer to prayer.

Next we turned to the adoption experts. I would no longer have to worry about what to tell the officer if I were ever caught speeding to another insemination, with the sacred sperm vial tucked in my bra.

We selected Bethany Christian Services and started pulling together reams of paperwork: medical and financial records; family histories and foster care certifications; first aid certifications and references. I highlighted our most attractive features for our adoption profile, much like the marketing fliers I used to prepare in hopes of winning textbook "adoptions."

I gathered our most baby-friendly photos, added hand-drawn decorative borders around each page for good measure, and sent the package off via Federal Express overnight morning delivery.

The next afternoon the phone rang. We had already been chosen by a birth mother—on her first trip to the agency. "Would you be interested in a match meeting?" our social worker asked.

After attending an adoption panel, Sam and I had decided on open adoption, where both parties meet in advance and decide on a birth plan together. In driving to meet our son's birth mom for the first time we felt the excited jitters of a blind date; both parties hoped for the right chemistry, but neither knew what to expect. What do you wear when you are about to meet the person who is planning to entrust her child to you? Do you go for casual or conservative; hip or traditional? For our first meeting, I settled on a flowered silk long-sleeved shirt and a short cotton navy blue skirt with red pumps.

Sam and I survived the two-hour drive to the adoption agency office in Modesto and recovered time lost in a shortcut. We breezed into the office and I was relieved that Elizabeth, the young woman sitting before us, looked just like the picture that she had mailed in advance: an angel dressed in soccer cleats. Liz loved the fact that I played soccer also. I loved the fact that she was proud of her Irish heritage and so sure the baby would be handsome. Thus we decided to call our son Kyle, which means *handsome* in Gaelic.

Liz never wavered in her convictions in making a plan for her son, but I told her that if she felt differently after spending time with the baby, we wanted her to raise him. We wanted to receive this gift with her full blessing; it was a lifelong decision. Knowing we cared for her as a person made the choice easier to bear, and we honored that bond by giving our son her middle name.

Three weeks later my beeper went off while I was at work. Trembling with excitement, I could barely dial the number, so the secretary grabbed the phone from me and called Liz's mom. "It's TIME!" I informed Sam. "For what?" he replied. Fortunately the nurses had administered drugs to slow down the labor, giving us time to rush home and drive down to Central California at the peak of rush hour. I refused to allow Sam to exit the freeway after he consumed too many cups of coffee; with the sweat pouring from his forehead, you would have thought he was the one giving birth.

We chatted with Liz between contractions who impressed me even more for hitting all the right answers on *Jeopardy* while enduring labor—without an epidural.

I cringed with empathy as the intensity of her contractions increased; my heart ached for the searing pain she was enduring on our behalf. Somehow I felt as if I should be in her place. The rapid, steady sound of Kyle's heartbeat from the monitor comforted me, as we waited for him to exit the birth canal. I stared in wonder when our purple-faced son entered the world and marveled that a petite teen could carry eight pounds and ten ounces of baby. Kyle's color quickly turned to a healthy pink as I cut the umbilical cord that connected him to his birth mom.

With tears streaming down our faces, two former strangers—now bonded as mothers—insisted that the other hold the baby first. Sam waited outside at a safe distance, only to come in during the dispelling of the afterbirth.

When we were being discharged from the hospital the following morning, this mature teenager insisted on signing all the release papers first, so that Sam and I could feel like the parents right away. The hospital social worker did not know what to make of this open adoption and kept reminding Liz that she "did not have to go through with this." With the private agency we used, the mom typically chooses to relinquish shortly after birth; the father can do so before the birth.

When Sam and I first received "the gift that lasts a lifetime," as Kyle's birth mom described him, I could hardly wait to share this amazing gift with others. Upon hearing that we were planning to stay in touch with the birth mom, well-meaning people expressed concern over what kind of weird co-parenting arrangement we were planning.

"Won't your child be confused as to who his real mother is? What if she wants him back?"

How many times have you received a gift, and the giver asked you to return it?

Upon leaving the hospital, friends of the birth mom asked her, "How can you give up your flesh and blood to strangers?"

Liz hated the tabloid-type implications that she would be staking out in our bushes ready to snatch her baby back. In the weeks preceding or following the birth, she *did* have the right to change her mind, but it is rare that the baby is "returned" once placement is made.

Would I rather not receive the gift than risk losing it?

The biological route to parenthood seemed a far riskier emotional investment, but no one asked, "What if you lose another pregnancy?"

Strangers did offer bizarre queries like, "What if you get a lemon?" As if adopting a child is like inheriting someone's second-hand car.

The best question of all was at our infant care class when the instructor asked us when our baby was due and we said, "In two weeks." We received many curious stares, as I was so clearly not pregnant and all the other mothers-to-be looked as if they could pop at any moment.

It is difficult to appreciate the joys of open adoption unless you have traveled the journey yourself. Many fears can be alleviated beforehand and either party can choose to pull out before the birth if the "match" does not feel right. Instead of worrying about what could go wrong, we relished everything that went right.

I loved that I could see so much of our birth mom in our son— from his pointed eyebrow expressions to his love for theater, his ease at meeting new people to his incredible sense of direction.

We spent several weekends bonding together, even spending a weekend together in a cabin near Yosemite, near the lake where she had loved camping as a child. It was our appreciation for the outdoors (and for dogs) that attracted our birth mom to us.

The last time we saw her was when Kyle turned seven. He wanted to know that his birth mom still cared for him. She chose not to stay in touch once she started a family of her own. Still, the gift of my son is one that will truly last a lifetime. He lifts me up when I am down and he is never too shy to say "I love you!"

Waiting for Sunshine—Surprises Come to Those Who Wait

Our son Kyle has always been good at speaking his mind and began requesting a baby brother at the age of two. Within the next six months I pulled the paperwork together and sent it off to the adoption agency. Remembering how quickly our first profile was selected after being mailed via Federal Express overnight delivery, I chose UPS Blue two-day air.

We waited a week, a month, and another month. Over a year later we were still waiting. I longed for overnight delivery! We sat through one false start and stall after another. The longer we waited the more options we checked off on the adoption forms. We had little control in the fertility process whereas with adoption we were faced with myriad choices—from ethnicity to disabilities to drug and alcohol exposure.

In waiting out uncertain times, it has sometimes felt like we would be stuck in one spot forever. I fear lack of control and want instant results, whether that is a dream house, a job, or a baby. But then the road opens wide, the way is made clear, and the light turns green again. These stretches would likely not seem as sweet without the hand-wringing moments I experienced along the way.

Once our son Nico arrived I understood the reason for the delays. Life may take us on a different route than originally planned, but if we aren't paying attention we can miss the road signs altogether.

On the day "THE CALL" came from Bethany Christian Services, our adoption agency, I had forgotten to switch the phone from fax to phone mode. For twelve months we wondered if Kyle would ever have a sibling and if a birth mother would ever choose us again. Like anxious homeowners listing their beloved home on the market, we hoped for the right person to pick our profile from the selection book.

Our ever-calm adoption counselor Sangeeta was trying to deliver the "Are you sitting down?" news. *Beep, beep.*... She dialed over and over, receiving nothing but busy signals. We did not possess a cell phone then so she turned to other technology.

"Please call me by 1:15PM or at home after 3PM," the fax read; then an e-mail popped up on our computer screen: "I can't get through on your phone. Please call me today." Something was up! Would we soon have another baby, or would this feel like another "false labor?"

We thought we were about to have a baby a few months earlier. I was recovering from a three-week bout of flu, when the phone woke me up. "Would you be open to a two-month-old girl—part African-American, Asian, and Indian?" our social worker asked. Leaping out of bed I croaked, "Sure! She sounds beautiful." We were thrilled to be considered, until the birth parents switched to a larger agency that offered them more couples to choose from.

A few weeks later a partnering agency called to inform us that an Indian couple was thinking seriously about choosing us. They decided to raise the baby themselves.

A Bethany branch office in the Seattle area called to say that we were "the perfect outdoor-type family" their young client was looking for. Would the third time be the charm? I waited on pins and needles to hear back from the agency. The teen decided against adoption and my hopes were dashed again.

I prayed for each of these moms-to-be and the impossible choices they faced, and at the same time I tried to imagine who our baby would be. Glancing at a biracial couple in the park with a bright-eyed, curly-haired daughter I wondered, would my baby look like that? Or would our baby have fair skin and freckles like Kyle?

"When can I have a little brother?" our four-year-old continued to plead.

After a roller coaster year I began to wonder whether we were meant to adopt another infant. Was God testing my patience or just holding out for the right baby to come along? Or did He envision a different path for us altogether? Scenes of chubby-cheeked infants smiling adoringly into their mother's eyes kept popping into view. I would look the other way.

Sam and I opened our minds to older children and attended information sessions, where we heard heart-wrenching tales about the children available in local foster-adoption and overseas programs. Soon thereafter I received a packet of information in the mail from an agency hosting Russian orphans for the summer. Each page displayed pictures of precious children. The kids would be introduced to local sponsor families in hopes of being selected for adoption.

Sam and I pored over photos and the same two little girls leapt off the pages. "Is this a sign?" I dialed the agency.

Several families had expressed interest in the same girls. "Would you be open to an older sibling group?" the adoption counselor inquired. This was too big a leap for us—we weren't ready to be outnumbered. *Should we abandon this dream?* My faith billowed about like a rowboat caught in a hailstorm.

I phoned our social worker and asked her to put our adoption plans on hold until further notice. I reasoned that if we were not in the profile book I could not be disappointed by not being chosen.

One night I attended a concert in which my niece Charlotte performed a solo in *The Prince of Egypt*. The words "I believe in miracles" pierced my soul and I wondered, *Do I...?*

That evening I surrendered: "Lord, I know you can make a miracle happen and I trust your plan for my life." I gave up my desire for a second child and praised Him for all He had already given me.

A few days later Sangeeta's note inched its way out of the fax machine.

"Do you want to pursue this?" she asked. "The baby is due in three weeks."

How could I say no?

"How did she find us?" I inquired.

Another Bethany social worker had accidentally left behind a section of the profile book—including a few of our pages—while visiting a young woman three months before. We were chosen when we weren't even officially available. No matter how much I try to write my own script, God shows me who is really in charge. The miracle of my son Nico's birth reminds me that we are all loved and chosen by Him!

Nico's birth mom, Colleen, wanted us to come to the hospital after the grand finale occurred. Fittingly, Nico was due on the fourth of July. A week later, Sam's parents and siblings flew into town from around the country for a family reunion that I had booked a year before. Despite a natural penchant for punctuality, Nico still showed no signs of arriving. We departed with the Linton clan for Stillwater Cove Ranch, a farm originally homesteaded in the 1860s and later converted to a boys' school and a guest ranch. The property, located on the coastal Highway 1 two hours north of San Francisco, had no telephones for guests and no cell reception.

Just as we finished unpacking our bags the next morning the manager came trotting up to our cabin, phone in hand, announcing "The baby is coming!"

The adoption counselor and the labor and delivery nurse both said we could take our time but we threw our clothes back into our duffel bags, dropped Kyle off at his grandmother's cabin, and jumped in the car. We were careful not to hit the straying lambs and peacocks as we crunched down the gravel driveway and hurried off to Central California. Somewhere along the Richmond Bridge crossing San Francisco Bay our baby was born. The nurse would not divulge the sex over the phone.

Upon reaching the maternity ward she informed us that Colleen was resting after complications from an emergency C-section, then kindly gave us a duplicate set of newborn footprints and a tour of the delivery room. Nico demonstrated hints of a stubborn streak immediately at birth, resisting natural contractions, vacuum extraction, and forceps. As psyched as we were to meet the feisty little guy we passed on the offer to take a peek so that Colleen could spend time with him first. We celebrated at the finest restaurant in town, Denny's, the site of our original "match meeting."

We checked into the only motel with vacancies, which smelled strongly of curry, and alerted Sam's family of the latest developments. The lodge manager delivered the following telegram-style message: "Baby born after 23-hour labor and C-section. Mom has not yet seen baby. Yvonne will call back between 9 and 10AM. It's a BOY!"

In the morning we bonded with our bright-eyed baby, wondering if we would get to take him home. Nico followed the movements of everyone around the room, not wanting to miss any of the action. Four days later we loaded our son into his car seat and drove out of the hospital parking lot, as the image of his waving birth mom and grandma faded in the distance.

A week later I summed up the courage to call Colleen. In my most casual voice I asked, "Are you doing okay, and were you able to sign the adoption papers?" I was glad that my thumping heart could not be heard over the telephone wires.

"Oh yeah, I sent the forms off today," she replied in the carefree tone of a teenager.

I hung up the phone crying tears of joy, then went to celebrate with Sam's parents who "coincidentally" were in the area for both our sons' births—trips that had been planned long beforehand. God has the perfect timing! When Nico turned two months old, Colleen asked to spend an afternoon with him, so I checked with the agency to ensure this was a reasonable request. She enjoyed several hours celebrating his young life with her closest friends while I took her mom out to lunch. It was her way of saying goodbye.

A month later she offered Nico a final farewell gift at a Round Table Pizza restaurant. When Nico wailed for me from across the large room, his voice reaching all the way to the bathroom stall, I knew I was his mom.

Our bond had been sealed when he was nineteen days old and a virus transformed our cheerful baby into a distraught patient in Stanford's Neonatal Intensive Care Unit. Upon his discharge, my friend Kathy enlightened me on a "supplemental nursing system." This is where you attempt to fool the baby into nursing, by strapping a small flask of milk around your neck and taping a plastic tube to your nipple to simulate nursing. Nico's little face lit up like a firecracker when she lifted her shirt to demonstrate. He knew exactly what to do. This must be why the delivery nurse had called him "the boob man." Nursing calmed him through any form of stress, until three months of age when he ditched the boob and started going straight for the tube. I had never planned to nurse but that was another blessing that God added to make my "birth story" special.

Of course, I grieved for the children I would never bear and ached for the loss these teen moms had experienced. I delighted in sharing with them the joys of my sons' first years through letters and photos. They are no doubt the most documented infants in history.

As with any relationship, I learned to respect boundaries with our birth mothers. When their life circumstances grew more complex and they both chose not to stay in touch, I prayed that we made a positive contribution in each of their lives. Knowing that we helped them to heal gave meaning to my fertility struggles. How sad that many adoptive parents elect to avoid initial contact for fear of a lifetime of required communication and commitment. I treasure the information I have about my children's birth families and the days we spent together. While creating my family required a little help from others, my children are as "natural" as any I may have delivered myself. And Kyle finally received the brother he so desired. (I occasionally must remind him that this is something he asked for!)

I understand now why I had to wait so long to become a mother and I see how my sons have brought sunshine into my life. They keep me grounded when clouds are gray, and they keep me company when I am on the road again.

3 ⊛ Find the Right Partner

Shopping Is a Hazardous Sport—Shopping with Children

There are two things to avoid doing solo when first becoming a mother: driving and shopping. These activities are usually best done in the presence of a fun friend, sister, or mom. In my sleep-altered excitement over parenthood I rushed out to do both. When I heard that Nico would soon be born, I found myself in a K-Mart parking lot at 9:30 one night hauling a sack stuffed with extra diapers and wipes, bottles and formula. A decent mother should be fully equipped for her new arrival, even with minimal notice.

In preparation we had upgraded to a minivan, dusted off the old infant car seat, and wiped the seatbelts of Kyle's former drool stains. The vehicle still sported a temporary plate and registration papers taped to the windshield, as we had driven it off the dealership lot the day before. It was so new I hardly remembered what it looked like as I scanned the packed parking lot. Row by row, I checked each car. I sought the aid of store security; they in turn summoned the police. Within minutes a cruiser rolled into the parking lot with lights flashing.

"What is the make and color?" the officer inquired.

It's a Nissan Quest, a sage green color," I guessed. His partner sauntered off to search for it. Minutes crawled by as the last of the shoppers trickled out the store, followed by a scattering of employees. Now the parking lot showed more concrete than car. That was when I caught a flash of red out of the corner of my eye. Now I remembered: our new van had not been filled with gas since it left the lot on a near-empty tank and was sitting safely in our driveway. I had to swallow my pride as I explained to the officers I had actually driven a different car—our red Mazda. "And there it is!" I pointed. Accustomed to dealing with deranged people, they graciously accepted my explanation. I drove off quickly before they committed me to a home for the bewildered.

Once Nico was born I rushed off to Costco right before closing time to retrieve the eagerly awaited first hospital photos and to restock on diapers. I had just spent four anxious days in the hospital waiting for his birth mom to recover from a grueling delivery and to confirm her adoption decision. Now I was relieved to be in a familiar Costco store, proof that life was returning to "normal."

I made a beeline for the photo rack and flipped through them, my skin tingling with emotion. Then my mind jolted back to reality so I tossed the packages in my empty cart and wandered off to grab the diapers and wipes, straying briefly from the cart. Eying the long check-out lines, I positioned my cart in the shortest one. As I was unloading my purchases, I discovered the photo envelopes were missing.

"Someone took my baby photos!" I wailed to the store clerk.

She translated this to "Someone took my baby!" This provoked a flurry of confused concern and alarm until I calmed everyone down and told them the photos were missing, not the baby. I was able to find my original cart with the photo envelope, parked right where I had abandoned it.

Over time I started taking the kids along on my shopping excursions for added excitement. One day I was perusing the aisles at Payless for new shoes for Kyle, our soon-to-be kindergartner. I figured this would be a short outing so I'd left the diaper bag behind. Glancing at twelve-month-old Nico waddling toward the shoe rack, I noticed his bulging diaper was sagging towards his ankles. Nico toddled forward and my eyes glanced past his pants toward the floor. To my horror, I discovered several suspicious cookie-shaped blotches on the carpet. Cautiously, I pried back the elastic waistband of his trousers and peered inside. Shades of similar brown seeped down his leg. I sprang into action and commanded big brother to "Stay right where you are and watch the carpet!"

In his practical way, five-year-old Kyle asked, "Why am I guarding poop?"

I herded the little perpetrator into the restroom, mercifully only a few yards away. I grabbed damp paper towels and wiped the streaks dripping down Nico's chunky legs, then hurried back to erase the evidence from the shoe department.

On my knees in the store, furiously scrubbing away, I cleared up the last spot on the carpet just as a salesperson approached the aisle.

"May I help you?" she asked casually.

"No thanks!" I snapped as I lobbed the soiled paper into the nearest trashcan, scooped up my fragrant son, and made a dash to the car. That was when I looked down and discovered that my beige pants were covered in dark brown poop. The air was rather pungent on the ride home. I learned that a spare diaper is more important than a spare credit card.

On a quest to pick up my car after its first annual maintenance, I ventured off to the dealer with stroller in tow. No more than two hundred yards out the door I ran into trouble. Since the traffic lights were not convenient to where we needed to cross, I chose to walk across several lanes of traffic instead.

With my luck a policeman showed up right in front of us, stopped his vehicle in the middle of the road, angled it to one side, and exited the driver's side. Like Moses parting the Red Sea, he walked toward me and raised his uniformed arms authoritatively, halting traffic in both directions. Averting my eyes in embarrassment, I pushed the stroller across the street as Kyle hurried alongside. Upon reaching the other side I waited to thank the officer for his help.

After waving the lines of cars forward, he approached us on the sidewalk with a stern demeanor and proceeded to lecture me for putting my children's lives in danger.

"You should get a ticket for jaywalking," he chided me. I awaited further tongue-lashing and punishment as I absorbed the criticism. The officer made a decision to grant reprieve when he detected my look of guilt and shame.

"I'll let it go just this time," he said dramatically.

I humbly thanked him for his grace, declaring, "I would give my life for my kids."

"Prove it to me!" he challenged but I quickly backed away before he held me to it.

The event is forever seared in my memory and Kyle's. That was the last time we ever jaywalked.

Another time the boys and I went shopping for a present at Toys-R-Us. We were just driving out the parking lot when we were summoned over by a familiar spinning cherry-topped sedan.

My heart pounded through my chest as I contemplated how I could talk myself out of a crime I did not know I had committed. What did I do wrong, except make the mistake of taking two tired kids to Toys-R-Us and not even come out with a purchase?

The officer turned to me and asked in a somber tone, "Do you know that your left brake light is burnt out?"

"I didn't know that," I declared innocently and thanked him for looking out for us, praising God that I would not have to face a day in traffic school.

When Counting Sheep Isn't Enough—Adventures in Sleeplessness

There is nothing like sleep deprivation and newborn babies to dull the senses. How can their sweet musical voices sound like a car alarm when they call to you in the dead of night? For a while I assumed that becoming a mother led to my erratic nocturnal schedule but then recalled that I have been operating with a sleep deficit long before my children began waking me in the night. *Or was it a snoring bed partner who was first to blame?*

I flashed back to eighth grade. My ability to drop off mid-task was legendary. One particularly droll high school teacher once turned to my twin with a dramatic roll of the eyes when his history class (taught in French) lulled me to sleep once more. I peeled my face off my plastic desk to find my pen still poised for action, and a circle of classmates snickering down at me. It took me years to recover from the trauma and come to realize that I truly do love history.

Since that humiliation, I have drooled upon many notebooks in college as well. I had to rely on the orderly notes of friends when my handwriting trailed off into undecipherable lines and squiggles that resembled a Richter scale more than a lecture outline. (Despite these lapses I managed to maintain top grades and complete college in three years.)

I figured my sleep patterns might return to normal after the thrill of graduating. Then, while visiting with my friend Rachel and her neighbors after work one evening, I nodded off to dreamland in mid-conversation. This offended her guests who assumed I did not find the company riveting enough to remain conscious.

One might assume the excitement of travel would stir the senses. Yet on one overseas flight I fell asleep before the plane left the runway. Another time Sam and I were driving from Dayton, Ohio, where he worked at Wright Patterson Air Force Base. We were on our way to visit Sam's sister Beth in Chattanooga, Tennessee and our mode of transportation was a Yamaha 350 motorcycle. This was early in our marriage and I could not figure out why Sam kept whacking his palm against my kneecap so unromantically. He was simply trying to revive me whenever my helmet clonked against his as I nodded off while zooming down the freeway at sixty miles per hour.

After moving to California and starting a family, I progressed from not being able to stay awake to not being able to fall asleep. When behavior modification techniques failed to bring about discernible results, and the temporary sleep deprivation therapy of a newborn baby no longer did the trick, I turned to the medical world for help. Lured by glowing testimonials of restored sleep patterns, I signed up for a sleep study that revealed I had mild sleep apnea.

My health insurance approved the use of a CPAP machine (Continuous Positive Airway Pressure). First I had to take a class at a medical device company, a half-hour away. This was almost as painful as traffic school, but with less diversity. Here everyone was elderly, overweight, or Asian, except for the one young man whose wife joined him in the group for moral support.

"You must not be too tired," the instructor winked, nodding at the red-faced man's pregnant partner. The teacher then spent ten minutes explaining how to turn on the machine. By this time I was begging for relief. One haggard woman was so sleep-deprived that she immediately fell asleep upon finally adjusting her mask and starting her machine. I wondered how she performed her job as a real estate agent and was thankful never to tour with her.

Strapping on the silicone mask in my bedroom the first night after class, I felt like a rookie pilot gearing up for a crucial mission. My cockpit panel was an individually calibrated machine designed to monitor apnea episodes. The CPAP machine prevents breathing from being continually interrupted when the upper airway becomes relaxed, as muscles loosen during sleep. This avoids the reduction of oxygen, which prompts a person to arouse, sparing their partner the chore of nudging them awake.

When sinus congestion further restricted my ability to breathe, I opted for the full-face mask with attached humidifier to reduce the discomfort of dry compressed air blown into the face. The snorkel-like hose protruding from my forehead was a real turn-on for Sam, I'm sure. Fortunately I did not frighten everyone away at his family reunion or start rumors about what strange devices I was taking into bed with me.

One advantage of the droning machine is that it drowns out snoring (yours or the person sleeping next to you), eliminating the need to be banished from the bed during the night like a jilted lover. After three months, however, the mask became too unpleasant to tolerate for extended periods and I ditched the device. Some people swear by them as their most trusted bed partners. I was not one of them.

A year later, still suffering from a serious sleep deficit, I pondered my latest health dilemma. For years I had subjected myself to allergy shots for recurring sinus infections. Now it was my stomach that was in continual distress. Driving along a city street congested with Mother's Day diners, my mind drifted to what latest health food supplement or Internet product might solve my worsening digestive woes. Every well-meaning health layman had a quick-fix cure, from colonic cleanses to soil-based organisms. Doctors simply repeated, "Eat lots of vegetables and drink lots of water." I imagined growing gills and sprouting leaves from the copious amounts I now consumed. On my way to purchase the latest recommendations, aloe vera juice and flaxseed oil, I noticed too late the vehicle nearly parked in front of me on the road. In a split second I saw there was no way to avoid colliding with it. I swerved to reduce the full impact of hitting the car from behind and waited for the inevitable bang of metal against metal. After peeling my bruised forehead off the windshield, I checked the oncoming flow of traffic and coaxed my drivable but dented van to a nearby parking lot.

This adrenalin-soaring event caused me to seek a solution once and for all. I partnered with a new gastroenterologist and we came up with a treatment plan that brought relief. Once the digestive issues were treated, my stomach, sleep, and allergies all started to improve. I need only to recall my season of sleep studies and CPAP machines to make me grateful for each night of rest.

Now whenever the old nemeses flare up, I know what to do to stay on course. The key is to act as if you are not drained and to find out what recharges your batteries. The more energy is invested, the more seems to be returned. I surround myself with positive people who tickle my funny bone. On rare clock-ticking nights, lying in wait for the dreams and the dawn to come, I recall the words of one doctor: "Resting is almost as good as sleeping." As God sustained the Israelites on manna and water, I trust I will receive what I need to embrace one day at a time.

Snoozing on Command—A Night in a Spartan Sleep Clinic

While sleep is a problem that has never plagued my husband, it eluded me for about seven years until I found help from an unlikely source. Until then, I had come to rely on Sam like never before. The simple task of throwing a meal together or shuttling kids to school on time had become a chore of blown-up proportions.

Normally a high-energy, happy, and healthy person, I initially turned to natural methods. When the normal platitudes of avoiding caffeine or exercise soon before bedtime and drinking hot milk failed, I tried herbs. Calm Forte, Valerian, St. John's Wort, Melatonin, chamomile tea, and even Chinese herbs and acupuncture, I sampled them all. Moving on to drugs, I took turns with Tylenol PM, Ambien, Lunesta, and Trazadone (which left me with permanently buzzing ears). Eventually I lost confidence to perform the natural act of sleeping, as I pondered which pill to pop each night. My bed had become my most feared enemy. I tried to promote positive endorphins with a vengeance, bouncing to exuberant aerobics instructors, rollerblading up steep hills, and reading enough *Chicken Soup for the Soul* books to fill a library.

When a colonoscopy started looking like an attractive way to catch up on sleep, it was time to seek relief, so I went to the top: the

Stanford Sleep Center behavior therapy program. There, fellow zombies regaled each other with harrowing tales of sleepless nights, some poor souls having been driven there by friends from three hours away. I fled from the room and investigated a new sleep clinic closer to home.

Since there are over seventy million sleep-deprived Americans, I waited months for an overnight sleep study. Clutching an overnight bag, I rang the side door of the nondescript building, carefully following the instructions to hit the buzzer three times. Once I recovered from the clandestine atmosphere that resembled a gambling operation more than a sleep center, I allowed a lady in a white lab jacket to lead me to my quarters. I tried to stay positive but quickly surmised this was not going to be a night at the Ritz.

No velour bathrobes or freshly-baked cookies awaited me. The nightstand contained only medical paraphernalia to which I would soon be tethered in a tangle of colored wires. There was no symphony of ocean sounds streaming into the room to dull the senses. The clinical white walls were barren, save for the remains of a few empty hooks. Taped to the door was a list of Emergency Exit instructions. I was not surprised to learn that a few cowardly souls had ditched this den without even attempting to spend the night. A sleep study ranks right up there with root canals and childbirth, though clearly women in labor have less choice of fleeing the room.

Barely had I entered when a stack of papers was handed to me, and I was asked to fill out yet another survey on my sleeping habits. If you suffer from recurring insomnia, you will be asked to fill out interminable supplies of forms to document sleep—or lack thereof. You will be asked about stressful activities, your mood, the time you go to bed, the time you fall asleep, the time you wake up, rise, return to sleep, and, finally, when you get up for good. Sleep specialists always want to know such things, yet all this time they will tell you not to keep an eye on the clock.

Another contradiction is the advice to "catch up on your sleep deficit" while avoiding naps and keeping the same bedtime and wake-up times. I was a notorious night owl. Yet here it was only 8:30PM—I had barely dotted the last "i" on the survey—when the technician proceeded to feed wires down my pant legs. You were instructed to bring pajamas and toiletries, but offered no chance to use them. I rushed off to find the dimly lit restroom, passing other rooms of victims amid a maze of cubicles.

Upon returning, I was forced into a supine position and reattached to the tangle of wires. The nurse technician placed a strap around my head and chest, leaving briefly to exchange it with the better-fitting, non-obese model. At least that was one small consolation. With the new straps securely in place, she plastered electrodes on my scalp, chest, and legs. More wires were snaked down my extremities. I resembled an astronaut launching into orbit; I pictured a control panel on the other side of the wall monitoring my every move and snore. The hidden microphone was ready to record and a camera perched strategically overhead. From the opposite corner of the room an infrared light dangled ominously, so I could be constantly monitored in the dark.

A new lab coat entered the room, sporting a mane of flaming red hair. In her gloved hands was a coil of plastic tubing. She asked if I was "rrr-ready," rolling her "r's" in a thick Russian accent.

"Rrr-ready for what?" I asked. Had I been given the lead role in a B-rated science fiction flick?

After explaining the procedure, she commanded the aide to hold a wastebasket under my chin and to cover me with a plastic sheet "just in case." This was the optional portion of the study where they feed a plastic tube down the throat and into the esophagus. Upon seeing this device I developed an overwhelming urge to bolt and cower in the bathroom stall. After being unplugged and re-plugged with probes to visit the facilities again, we started over. "Don't forrrrce it," the technician rolled to the aide, demonstrating her technique. "If it becomes too much, say *nyet*!"

Despite repeated warnings about hurling, she continued to coax the wire down my right nostril. Each time it got "shtuck," she tried it again. We switched to the left nostril. When that one became too sensitive, she returned to the right one. After five tries she abandoned her efforts, much to my relief.

Thankfully it was time to crawl into bed. I carefully eased my torso down, pulling my trail of wires with me. Awkwardly I turned around to arrange the flimsy excuse for a pillow. Then I settled down to read, with one eye on the thermostat clock reminding me of how many minutes remained before the technician returned to hit the light switch. With the room now plunged into darkness and no night-light in sight, I was at the mercy of those listening in. The literature mentioned a "Call" button, but it was very cleverly disguised. Should I need anything, I would be forced to holler into the night and wait for help to magically appear. At least the electrodes were not cemented to my skull, though they shifted so easily the technician kept popping through the door to adjust them. The pressure to achieve sleep, to give the computer data to analyze, steadily mounted.

The bedding hardly invited shut-eye. A cotton sheet continually slipped off the crinkly plastic mattress cover, and the threadbare blanket offered as much comfort as the stamp-sized gowns nurses provide you at doctor's appointments. Lying awake in the required back position, I listened to the drone of a fan as it creaked from side to side, shuffling papers in its wake. Around 2:30AM, I finally asked the technician to silence the thing before I lunged up and tossed it out the window. Three hours later, I was awakened and unplugged from the assorted tracking devices.

The data showed that somehow I managed to sleep more than I had imagined. It also demonstrated that I had over three hundred restless leg movements, obstructed breathing, and that I had trouble falling into deep REM sleep and staying asleep. No wonder! I could hardly wait to bail from here and count sheep in the comfort of my own bed—before I was asked to fill out another survey. Though the surveys taught me nothing new, I learned the support of family and friends can be the best cure of all.

Living in the Lap of Luxury—When Two Cheap Friends Hit the Spa

My sour night at the sleep clinic was sweetened by the fact that I would soon be seeing my best friend Rachel. Friends have a way of making everything feel better—like moms, chocolate, and chicken soup. Rachel and I met over twenty years ago at Stanford University when Sam attended graduate school. Our friendship was forged over a banana.

Lacking this key ingredient for banana bread I had called up Rachel, who lived in the apartment three floors up. She sent a banana down to me on the elevator. Since then we have always been there for each other. While two states now separate us, our times together still resemble the old "*I Love Lucy*" comedy sitcoms. We take turns playing Lucy and her sidekick Ethel.

After earning her doctorate in genetics at the University of Washington, Rachel was invited to present a science paper at an international genetics symposium hosted by her previous boss at Stanford, a past Nobel Prize nominee. I was the non–science nerd invited along. Recognizing the wonderful opportunity that Sam would have to bond with our kids all weekend, I accepted her offer. Rachel and I made plans to meet at the Silverado Resort in Napa wine country, where we would sample local cuisine, courtesy of Bay Area pharmaceutical companies.

Valets seized my car when I drove up the circular drive to check in. I wondered when I would see my keys again and in what state I left the car. Numerous famous guests had frequented this building, including

Abraham Lincoln, Ulysses Grant, Andrew Jackson, and Theodore Roosevelt. I stood on hallowed ground.

Against emerald hills and threatening skies loomed a gleaming white edifice. An army of doormen greeted me at the door—a wonder of carved wood, flanked by a row of columns on each side. It was hard not to feel like royalty as bellmen sprang to swing open doors. I half-expected to wave to my subjects and nod to my entourage, but felt considerably less suave after a doorman swung a door into my boob as I stepped into the ornate lobby. With my chest deflated but my pride intact, I registered for our suite whose rate equaled that of my first apartment's monthly rent. I declined the offer of being driven there by a doorman in a golf cart, choosing to stroll along the course instead. Rachel greeted me at the door.

This was certainly a step up from my stays at Motel 6; there was a cover on the toilet seat here. No mints on the pillows but there was a pair of velour bathrobes in the closet and a wood-burning fireplace complete with Duraflame log. The kitchen, living room area, and bedroom area each had its own television, telephone, and mini-bar. The thought of spending $6 for honey-roasted peanuts quickly abated my hunger pangs. Rachel decided that checking her e-mails could also wait once we read about the extra Internet fees and energy surcharges. She had only recently crawled out from under a mountain of graduate school bills.

Being the lavish spendthrifts we are, we passed on manicures, body wraps, and massage services and opted for the free spa and sauna included in our room price. After unpacking our duffle bags we sought out the spa facilities, flanked by two stately palm trees and a spacious sky-lit entryway. We passed on the lap pools, deciding that might involve work, and chose to massage our muscles with the hot tub jets instead. We were joined by a couple who leaned back and closed their eyes in the calming steamy water. What heaven! Until, that is, Rachel stepped out to hit the Restart button.

The heat momentarily fogged her senses, preventing her from distinguishing the Emergency button from the jets. A high-pitched alarm immediately sounded, sending spa personnel scurrying in all directions in an attempt to silence it. The jacuzzi had become more a source of an embarrassment than relaxation, so we retreated to the indoor sauna—with her former laboratory partner in close pursuit. Strong in opinion but weak in directions, Rachel confidently led the way, oblivious to her colleague's gentle gestures in the opposite direction.

"That way," he suggested tactfully, to which she insisted, "This way!"

"No—that way!" he implored, his voice rising in urgency. While they debated the directions, I found the sauna. Talk about going from the frying pan into the fire. At least there were no jet buttons to re-activate.

We staggered out of the steam to retrieve the plush robes and plastic sandals provided and plodded to the women's room to change. Standing over our lockers I launched into a tirade about how people routinely spend that kind of money to indulge themselves. Rachel started frantically giving me the universal "Zip your lips" signal. Out of sight but not earshot, two robed women with a tower of hair and towels had just returned from a massage treatment. Rachel, trying to prevent our being mortified any further, practically shoved me out the door. I missed the chance to partake of the "comfort tea" and health snacks set up by the fireplace. But dinner awaited us at a nearby winery. Rachel felt ready for a drink at that point.

An hour later, we found ourselves being catered to again, this time in more formal wear. We had barely entered the establishment when wine glasses were thrust into our hands. Knowing I become tipsy at the mere suggestion of alcohol, Rachel ordered me to grab a glass and "just hold onto it." (Better not to draw any more attention to ourselves.) I found my glass being refilled before I even had a chance to pretend to drink from it. Replenished glasses in hand, we sauntered over to hear the wine-cellar tour. I gladly would have let the man wax eloquently for an hour in exchange for the free, five-course meal.

With full bellies, we returned hours later to our room and collapsed on our beds. We had come a long way since her first job as a lab assistant and my stint as a Stanford receptionist. Living in the lap of luxury was beginning to wear us out! Being casual types, we ditched the velour robes and pulled on our T-shirts and sweats. Rachel still had a genetics exam to grade for a class of anxious undergraduates back home in Seattle. With our priorities now properly readjusted, we decided that it could wait until morning—after the all-you-can-eat-breakfast and fresh-squeezed orange juice.

Weekend at the Spa

Left Behind—Beware of Zealous Biking Partners

I once accepted an invitation from my friend Rod to accompany him on a diabetes charity bike tour through the coastal hills of Santa Cruz County. He knew that I enjoyed biking for good causes, and this was his first venture of the sort. Rod was an avid biker but had been recently been diagnosed as diabetic and I figured he could use the moral support.

The day started inauspiciously. I tiptoed out of the house early to avoid waking Sam and the boys and drove my car to Rod's house. We arrived at the event site well before the 7AM start time. Glancing around the thin crowd, I relished the rare head start I was getting, and assumed everyone else must still be dozing in bed. Grabbing a bagel, I opted to skip the remaining breakfast selections. I believed that these rides are always well equipped, and I did not need any extra blubber bursting from my Lycra biking shorts.

I had been sufficiently humbled once before while completing a hundred-mile charity ride with my friend Cathy. While rolling through the mustard-covered hills of California's wine country, my model-looks friend asked me perkily from behind, "Have you lost weight? Your butt looks smaller!"

At one particularly scenic location a staff photographer approached us, asking us to pose in a variety of stances. Months later, I proudly opened a brochure from the Multiple Sclerosis foundation to find the scene from our impromptu photo shoot. Cathy's bronzed face and slimming biking jersey jumped off the glossy page. Eagerly I scanned the picture to see what had become of me. I had been obliterated! Just like that, I was sliced out like yesterday's news story.

So here I was, happily pedaling through the bucolic landscape of Santa Cruz County with Rod, admiring the vistas of towering oaks and ornamental grasses swaying in the wind. While the early ocean breeze cut through my thin jacket, I knew another twenty miles on the road would warm me up until the next rest stop. I began speculating about what sumptuous fare awaited us for our snacking pleasure.

Rod initially motored effortlessly beside me but leapt farther and farther ahead until disappearing from view. Had we been on a tandem, we would have stretched over two counties by now. *Not to worry; he'll be waiting at the rest stop.*

"This isn't bad so far," I said to a biker pulling up beside me. We chatted for a few minutes and maintained a comfortable pace, enjoying the draft off the cyclists in front of us. The Rest Stop signs started appearing at the side of the road, counting down the time that remained. I licked my lips in anticipation. Soon the refreshment table came into view. There stood Rod waiting for me in his sweaty biking jersey. At six-foot-five he was easy to spot.

I surveyed the spread and my stomach dropped in disappointment at the meager offerings. Pocketing a Power Bar for the road to sustain me until the next stop, I decided to push on.

"First I have to use the restroom," I told Rod.

"Go ahead," he assured me.

As I released my breath from the pungent Porta-Potty and scrubbed my hands with Purell, I scanned the landscape for a sign of Rod. A few more bikers trickled in. No large purple jersey leapt out of the thinning crowd. I gazed down the road and still saw no trace of him. The last of the bikers faded into specks on the horizon, prompting me to hop back on my bike and pump furiously to catch up. Soon they, too, were out of view. *Had Rod said, "Go ahead" or "I'm going ahead?"*

Eventually a support vehicle pulled up.

"Have you seen a tall guy in a dark purple jersey?" I asked the volunteer.

He promised to look out for him. "Only forty-five miles to go," he encouraged. Birds soaring above clucked down, either in sympathy or in mocking laughter.

"Where is everybody?" I huffed, chugging along a steep stretch of road in search of signs of life. Was I the sole survivor of an alien takeover, or had the Rapture occurred and I was the only one left behind?

After checking my dog-eared map for signs of another missed turn, I came across a cluster of bungalows and small commercial buildings. They may have been beauties in their day, but now looked ready to collapse with the next gust of wind. Still, it was like finding the lights of Vegas after being lost in the desert. I glanced hopefully for a head poking up from the sagging porches, or for a sign pointing to a taco stand. Only the shell of an old auto repair shop remained.

The next rest stop should appear in just ten miles, I comforted myself.

Gradually the flat stretch of strawberry fields gave way to steep hills. I eyed them longingly. Up I panted, dropping my gears to the lowest rung. The silence was broken by the grinding of the chain and the growling of my stomach.

The much-anticipated rest stop materialized into nothing more than a dot on the map. Due to lack of volunteer support it had never been set up. I wondered how desperate I would have to become to start begging by the side of the road. Finally I came upon an old country store, its sign long since faded in the California sun. Pulling my emergency dollar bills from my biking jersey, I waddled into the store like a cowboy. Within seconds I devoured a stale donut and an overpriced package of peanuts. I was forced to relinquish a third item when the pimply-faced teenage clerk showed no mercy at my five-cent deficit. Biking along, I stuffed the last salty remains in my mouth. I would not fare well on *Survivor* as I prefer instant gratification over cautious rationing.

Just when I had all but given up hope of spotting another rest stop, two hazy figures loomed in the distance. I plodded on. As I coasted up to the table, I eased my saddle-sore torso off the bike and surveyed the food.

Then it hit me.

I had twenty more miles to go through coastal hills and only a few orange rinds and bruised banana chunks remained. I knew that starving people overseas would drool over such succulent treasures. But having been spoiled with unlimited riches in the past, I could barely conceal my dismay. I grabbed a handful of fruit remnants and peddled on. I wondered if the ride was purposely ill equipped in order to simulate a diabetic blood sugar crisis.

The volunteer I had seen earlier pulled up on his Harley and asked if I needed anything. Spotting the scar on my leg, he asked, "Are you the one who was run over by a bus once? Your friend is waiting for you at the banquet."

This sounded almost religious, like the gospel tunes I sang as a kid. "He brought me to his banqueting table, his banner over me is love..." I was ready for the banner that said "Finish Line!"

Coming to a junction in the road, I had my chance to break away on a short-cut and shave miles off the route, or keep going on the marked path. I kept going. Mashing down my pedals into yet another revolution, over yet another incline, I fantasized about the juicy burgers and fresh salads that awaited me. I recalled the desperately poor villagers I had met in Haiti—and the many like them—who suffer each day to find nourishment. Due to the lack of support from wealthier nations, they arrive at the relief center full of hope, but leave with empty stomachs after the donations have run dry. Where do they find the strength to trudge on? When will *they* reach the banquet table?

Fortunately for me, relief was only a few miles farther down the road. Rod waited patiently, wondering if I had collapsed in a field of artichokes. He had gathered the cold remains of a salmon and burger barbeque with a few scraps of wilted lettuce leaves the side. Rather than reflect on how the food would taste even better warm and fresh, I relished the abundance of riches before me. As my blood sugar returned to normal, I gave thanks for all I had and vowed to think twice about biking with this speedster friend again. Rod's fanny pack still bulged with the remains of brownies his wife had lovingly baked. When I ran into her the following week she remarked, "Rod had a great time—he would love to ride with you again."

Sure—I'll pack my own food and meet him at the finish line! Or I'll stick with my mountain biking club, *Mere Mortals*, where riders wait for stragglers at the top of the hill.

Walk on the Wild Side—Sightseeing by Night

I have longed for the open road since the age of two when, like baboons, my twin and I would scale five-foot backyard fences with our diapers poking out from under our sundresses. We would seek every item in the yard to help us escape, whether a lawn mower, a ladder, or a teeter-totter pulled up to the fence. Our older sisters were continually commissioned to retrieve us.

Once I eventually settled down with a yard, home, and family of my own, my parents enjoyed coming to help me contain my accumulating domestic processions. Each visit was more productive than the last.

Their arrival is occasionally prefaced by frenzied attempts to whip the house into showroom condition, but they always find more work to do. Such industriousness calls for the proper reward, so whenever they come I treat them to a creative getaway. They share my appreciation for reading obscure historical plaques, unlike my kids, and have a much longer sightseeing threshold.

One year I chose a bed and breakfast in a former mine headquarters where they used to melt gold before loading it onto the stagecoaches. We explored nearby caves and wineries and found ancient Indian grinding stones. Another year I settled on a Victorian Inn further down Route 49 in California's gold's country. We clambered over river rocks by an old mill, climbed aboard an old steam engine train, and attended a top-rate performance in California's longest operating theater. Most recently we sampled Spanish missions and lodged in a Moorish-themed room on William Rudolph Hearst's former hunting estate, now an army base.

The most vivid outing is our hike through Calaveras Big Trees State Park. Off to an early start, I aimed the car in the direction of Yosemite, pulling out of the driveway at 11:30AM. After a whirlwind tour of local attractions along the way and "one more stop," we approached our final destination in late afternoon. I eagerly escorted my parents into the park entrance, home of the giant sequoia trees.

We shot right past the conveniently marked trail the ranger had recommended ("You can't miss it" were her exact words). Curving around miles of blurry pines and azure skies, we eagerly looked to see what lay beyond the next bend. After circling back towards the intended trailhead, I parked the car and we hurried over to the informational displays, where we educated ourselves on the history of the forests. We marveled at how one formerly 300-foot-high beauty could have been standing from the time of Christ—and how men could have chopped it down for a traveling tourist attraction in the late 1800s. Dad and I sauntered along, admiring these towering testaments of time. Mom, the practical one, eyed the graying sky suspiciously and suggested we turn back at Marker 7. To reassure her I reached into my back pocket where I had stuffed the trail map, but it had dropped out along the way.

"It's only about a mile and a half," I said. "How long could it take?" I talked her into continuing.

My mother was still a speed walker at seventy-six and she cajoled my dad and me to pick up the pace. Occasionally I checked back on my father to ensure that he had not been snatched by a mountain lion. My mom had seen wildlife warning signs at the trailhead while I was studying the route, and now she fully imagined what dangers lurked behind every tree.

Hurrying along the trail, we could not help but notice the markers rising higher ... and higher ... and higher. We bravely forged on farther and farther ... and farther. The ancient sequoias loomed over us like a row of evil giants, their treetops swallowed up by an ever-darkening sky. Bushes rustled mysteriously from both sides of the path. Finally, at the now-barely visible marker 26, we spotted a distant sliver of light. By this time the sun had disappeared without a trace, retired for the night.

My mom bolted towards the yellow glow streaming from the restroom, nearly wetting her pants in the process. There was certainly no lack of trees for those feeling the call of nature. By the time she exited the men's restroom (aren't they always the quickest ones to find?), a million stars winked down at us. I wondered who shut off the light, amazed at the speed at which the sky changed from bluish grey to black.

The ranger swung by with a large smile on his face, probably relieved that the stranded car now had an owner and he could go home for dinner instead of having to launch a search party.

I jogged back to retrieve a brochure so I could show my folks the terrain we had sprinted through in the dark. The suggested time to walk the trail was one and a half hours; we had taken twenty minutes. Since becoming a teacher, I have learned the art of scheduling activities and transitioning from one to the next. Should I forget this lesson, I have only to peer at the half-darkened photos of my day in the giant sequoias park. Is that my imagination or is that blur an animal lurking behind a tree? Never mind. It is probably just Dad running to catch up.

HELP: The Parents are Coming!—The Things They Do for Love

Parents. You have to give them credit. They try to improve our lives in countless ways to show they love us. They rush to our aid when we most need it (and even when we don't yet know we need it). And still we take them for granted. During one visit my dad helped me sand, prime, and paint the twenty-one kitchen cupboard doors that our hopeless handyman, Joe, had abandoned a year before. (More about Joe later.)

While Dad would meticulously sand away the remaining clumps of paint that I had stripped earlier, I would hack them off with a scraper. While he started with the trim, I saved it for last. When he had just the right amount of paint on his brush, I had too much or too little. His paint shirt remained spot-free while mine sported a layer of color.

Dodging flying chips and dripping paint, we steadily plugged away, hanging the last door on the eve of his departure.

My mother's specialty is laundry. She could clear the stains of a white football jersey after a mud brawl; my whites turn gray from overstuffing the washing machine. Any dirty deed is more fun with the right quarterback—or not. Facing a mountain of laundry on the couch, Mom bravely sorted through it all, one unmatched sock at a time. Tossing me a pair of underwear, she asked, feigning innocence, "These aren't yours, are they? They look awfully big but I didn't see the opening in front so I figured they must be yours." My ego dropped faster than a pair of briefs with tattered elastic. Now that she is away I can enjoy my oversized panties in peace, though they are no longer artfully arranged in the drawers.

Mom is so tidy that she runs the recycled glass jars through the dishwasher before setting them on the curb. After one of her recent makeovers our linen closet never looked more pristine. "Simple! Fold them this way in three crisp layers," Mom advised. Afraid to disturb the picture-perfect stacks, we secretly planned to use the same sheet and towel over and over. The kitchen cupboards were carefully rearranged. It took only a few weeks to put everything back.

"But it looks so much better this way, don't you think?"

"Yes, Mom!"

Out went my favorite picture from the garden window. "Too big," she decided. The plants now stood cloistered in the corner like a group of schoolgirls. Mom rearranged the cluttered portraits stuck to the fridge door by family group, in chronological order of niece and nephew.

"You really need a _____," my mom will often say; just fill in the blank. If she thinks we need it badly enough and we do not spring to purchase the item we have managed for twenty years to go without, she will buy it for us.

My father will set about repairing items that I have all but abandoned. ("If Noah could build an ark, I can fix this umbrella set!" he is quoted as saying.) A squeaky hinge, a loose bolt, a broken fence, a rusty tool; nothing escapes his loving attention.

While Dad quietly goes about making enhancements to our home, Mom will accompany her good deeds with admonitions to keep it up. "Don't let the laundry pile up. And don't let the plants dry out." She planted a trio of foxgloves whose drooping leaves now greet us daily in silent mockery. I may have to photograph all the flowers to recall what to replace before the next visit. My naturally neat mom fails to realize how easy it is for some to fall off the wagon with our routines. Like recovering addicts, we must continually resist our casual ways. They say it takes six weeks to establish a habit, but our family struggles to reach the six-hour mark.

Impromptu visitors typically prompt a flurry of activity on our part. Early in our marriage when my in-laws drove up a day early to visit us in our Stanford University apartment, I quickly sent Sam to intercept them, with instructions to park the car a mile away. Another time, when I sent him to pick them up from the airport, they thankfully encountered a stall on the way home. It bought me an extra half hour of emergency cleaning.

The kids know that having guests requires one day's advance warning.

"Can I invite so-and-so over today?" our sociable son Nico used to plead. "I promise I won't let him in the house." For years, the closest he got to a play date was when we gave classmates a ride home. The car was quicker to restore than the house when our intrepid housecleaner, Dina, was not available. Our boys thrilled at the prospect of Halloween because it was like having someone over each time the doorbell rang.

My parents' biannual fall visits are not only opportunities to see the grandchildren; they are home inspections. Now nearly in their eighties, my parents still have more energy than those half their age, God bless them. They are like Clydesdales horses: strong and reliable. Arriving after a twelve-hour flight from New Zealand, they immediately set to work sweeping our garage and stacking the discarded bricks at the side of our driveway into a neat little pile. I can now predict what items will attract attention and intentionally leave some out as bait. Sam once put tape on the floor to see if his favorite chair was moved. It was.

When visiting us, Mom leaves her signature everywhere. She can't help herself. After shaking the feeling of being a guest in my own home, I relish all the improvements that will surely result. This is far superior to the parents and in-laws who sit around waiting to be entertained. Such is the fate of a friend who must endure comments like, "You have a dull neighborhood." Or, "Today I counted the number of leaves in your yard." My parents don't have time to be bored; they keep themselves too busy. They *earn* their sightseeing breaks.

The important thing is to appreciate the industriousness and not to take suggestions as personal criticisms. Finally, I came to realize that parents pitch in to show us they love us, not to point out our shortcomings. A casual home does not imply domestic disaster or moral failing. We just have different priorities and ways of doing things.

My mother will plan any dinner of more than two place settings weeks ahead of time. Ingredients are carefully pre-selected and stocked, ready for action. The table will be artfully arranged. (For large crowds, nameplates might be assigned.) Decorations adorn the table. At our home, the table is being set up as the guests are walking up the driveway, after the boys have been bribed with imaginary allowances. Plastic placemats are replaced with a clean tablecloth and a strategically placed candle. The menu is what happens to be in the fridge if I did not have time to shop in advance.

One of my most successful Christmas dinners was for a group of thirteen people, a mouth-watering fare of Moroccan and French cuisine, whipped together from a handful of ingredients. My specialty is creating culinary masterpieces from scratch at a moment's notice. I can set five fresh dishes on the table in an hour or less. Mom views this as nothing short of miraculous. While she is Julia Child in the kitchen, she thinks I am a magician. The art of cooking is recipe selection, improvisation, and shortcuts—and a good frying pan.

Though I have lived away from home for years my mom still wants to leave her maternal mark and pass on her wealth of domestic tips. It is never too late to learn new tricks. With each additional task completed, I vow to do better next time. Their visits evoke more preparation than an episode of *Extreme Makeover: Home Edition*. Two hours until the parents come home!

No matter how old we are, perhaps we never stop trying to please our parents. I even swept the front walkway the last time they came. The car was cleared of abandoned water bottles and gum wrappers, the garage cleaned up, and a few more inches of closet space relinquished. Clutter was carefully stashed away and my mom's past gifts were prominently displayed. I gave myself a B+. Maybe their next visit will earn an A.

The "Helpful" Handyman—The Joys of Home Improvement

My hubby deftly tackles problems at work and at home but a handyman he is not. At least he knows when he needs a hand, avoiding the endless half-finished projects that other wives endure. Rather than subject my parents to more work projects on their next visit, Sam has no problem paying someone to do the job.

So along came Joe.

I originally called Joe to restore our bathroom to its pre-flood condition, and then called him back to breathe new life into our aging kitchen. This would involve stripping twenty cabinet doors of forty years of paint and staining them.

At first Joe oozed confidence and plunged into his project with the enthusiasm of a coach preparing for the World Series.

"I have a friend who can whip these doors through a machine and have them stripped in no time," Joe declared.

I flinched at the word *strip* after my twin sister's scare with a horny handyman who was only interested in one form of payment. I was willing to let Joe's friend strip my doors but somehow neither the friend nor the machine ever materialized. Joe tackled the doors by hand. Soon the work started slowing down, as if his battery juice was running low. Or perhaps he was running on other kinds of juice?

I began to feel trapped, always wondering when he would return, but not trusting him with a spare key. Whenever Joe rolled up the driveway I resisted the urge to ask, "How long are you going to stay this time and will I ever see you again?" His pickup truck was so fickle that he spent more time coaxing it here than he spent working. After puttering around in the kitchen for a few minutes, his arm would raise in a friendly farewell. Even the patience of Job would wear thin with Joe.

One time, thinking he was long gone, I sank into the bubbles of my private outdoor jacuzzi. As I was starting to unwind and enjoy the vibration of the jets pulsing against my neck, I heard my name summoned from above.

Joe spoke sheepishly through the backyard fence, "Can you give me a jump?"

I grabbed a towel to wrap around my hot pink bathing suit and trudged to the driveway. While peering under the hood of the truck, I was approached by my neighbor.

"What are you doing?" Annemarie inquired.

I resisted saying, "What does it look like?" and replied, "I'm helping out the handyman."

Arching her eyebrows in my direction, she said, "Dressed like that?"

This was the same person who gave me a one-page-calendar with twelve positions of endearment, one for each month of the year. It was being used as a bookmark in my Bible. Sadly, I do not refer to either as often as I should.

We went on vacation and Joe attacked our cabinets with gusto. He stripped and stained one whole cabinet door. Or rather, part of a door. The rest he brought home with him to finish in his spare time.

One day (when Joe's truck was actually running) he called with news. "A power line fell on my way over and it is completely blocking the road. There was no way to get past it, so I had to go home." Detecting a hint of skepticism in my voice, he added, "You can call the power company and check for yourself." He had already exhausted all other plausible excuses so I did not doubt him.

When Joe needed time off to tend to his ailing mom, I initially oozed with compassion. Months went by. Upon returning from Pennsylvania he told us, "I have this great new business idea..." I never expected to see him again.

One day he appeared on my doorstep like a ghost of Christmas past. His holey T-shirt sported stains of sweat. In the back of the truck lay a rusty mountain bike. He lugged this alternate mode of transportation around with him in the event that his truck choked up and died. Since he lived an hour away by car and his closest neighbors were horses and sheep, this was optimistic at best. The neighbor's mule might have made better time than his wheels. Still, I applauded his efforts.

He immediately went to work, though sadly most of the supplies he needed were at home in his converted barn. This necessitated another trip to Home Depot. "I'll be back in a jiffy," he called out cheerfully as he disappeared in a trail of smoke.

An hour later, since Joe did not believe in cell phones, I drove to Home Depot to seek him out. As I was scanning the parking lot, the day laborers all hustled toward my car in hopeful anticipation. I quickly departed to search nearby gas stations and repair shops. No sign of Joe. I left messages at his home. In the morning I received the now-routine, contrite explanation. Joe had been overcome by dizziness and had driven himself to the closest Veteran's Hospital. After that he navigated the winding roads to his hovel an hour away and collapsed into bed, not crawling to the phone to retrieve messages until morning. I detected a slight slur in his voice and wondered if alcohol was a good antidote for dizziness.

"I had a few beers," he admitted. He offered to have us over for a family barbecue when he felt better. All I wanted was my cabinets finished in time for my birthday. In the event that I would have to instigate a rescue operation for my cabinet doors, I casually requested his address.

It did not come to that. The crimson leaves of fall gave way to the empty branches of winter and the prospects for completing the work grew increasingly grim.

After another failed attempt to coax more work out of Joe, I realized I had given him more chances than God gave the Israelites. At this rate, it would take forty years for my kitchen to be finished. I suggested he return the pieces of our kitchen to us. He agreed and, true to his word, he showed up on my front porch with a pile of cabinet doors.

"You're fired!" the kids announced and he laughed, assuming they had been viewing reruns of *The Apprentice*.

Months later I was still trying to finish the work myself and began to see why Joe's enthusiasm for the project had plummeted with each passing day. Nico, our budding builder at age seven, offered to assemble new ones as he had with the garage cabinets. But I elected to repaint the doors until we could eventually replace them.

The jury is still out on when our home will be finished "improving." But if anything breaks down, I am not going to be the one to fix it. And neither is Joe.

Out with the Old, In with the New—Be Careful What You Wish For

An unexpected work bonus from Sam's biotech employer enabled me to finally renovate the kitchen in the way I had always dreamed. I sought and received Dad's blessing to gut the same cabinets he and I had so painstakingly refurbished two years before. When I contacted the reliable contractor who had completed our family room addition, he took one glance at the cryptic sketches I had received from the local cabinet shop and that was the last I saw of him, leaving me with a house full of cherry-stained cabinets and no one to install them.

I was picking up Nico from school one day and decided on impulse to show him the new tile work adorning a house near the school. Nico loves to create things and I wanted to encourage his artistic eye.

A stylish sixty-year-old stepped out the door. "Can I help you?" he asked. Little did Enrique imagine where his innocuous query would lead him.

After conversing for several minutes I learned that Enrique was the inspiration behind his home's custom touches and that he remodeled homes for a living. How fortuitous! We talked, I checked out a few of his references and recent projects, and I hired him.

A week later he went to work ripping out all traces of my former kitchen. Three weeks of microwave cooking later he completed it. I finally had new cabinets—just in time for my birthday. He even brought flowers to decorate the new countertop.

Enrique managed to combine two small, impractical rooms into one beautiful kitchen and made me promise not to bury his handiwork with dirty dishes. I wish I could say I have always kept that promise.

As Enrique has completed more projects for me over the years, our friendship has grown. Then he started to notice other areas of the house. Spotting the stack of magazines for a potential art project sitting on a shelf in our garage he asked skeptically, "When's the last time you looked at those? Or slept on that extra mattress? Get rid of it! I'll bring my truck over."

He moved on to the side yard. "Do you still use the windsurfing boards? How about that kayak?" He was relentless.

Following a trail of bikes back into the garage, he quizzed "Do you really need four laundry baskets?"

Laundry is my nemesis. I'm not sure how so many socks and shirts even accumulate since the boys wear the same outfit for a week; they must reproduce at night. I wanted to tame this monster once and for all, and Enrique jumped into action when Sam and I asked him to convert our laundry area into a more efficient space.

When he was through, he told me, "I'm going to come back to check on you," like a doctor making house calls.

True to his word, Enrique appeared on my doorstep one week later to gauge my progress. If this were my mother I might have taken offense, but Mom was grateful that someone else had taken on the challenge of preventing me from becoming a clutter queen. Somehow I had managed to find a handyman, designer, and life coach all wrapped into one.

Noticing my various sports-related paraphernalia, he inquired about my exercise habits. Enrique was a former professional soccer player who knew a thing or two about self-discipline. Now he was going to whip me in physical shape? Okay, maybe it was time to find a new contractor. Instead I elected to master all my New Year's Resolutions at once and faced my fitness goals with renewed fervor. I even accepted the help of a trainer.

"You need me!" he implored.

How could I say no?

It's arduous to establish new routines but my family has enjoyed the resulting benefits.

"All I want is a clear path through the house," my low-maintenance spouse will say. But he appreciates being able to park his motorcycle in the garage again, not having to sidestep game cartridges on the living room floor, and finding clean clothes in his drawer every day. He no longer resorts to wearing my jeans—one should never marry a man with the same pants size. The kids no longer wait until the housecleaner comes to tidy their rooms, even when no one is coming over.

We all need someone like Enrique in our lives to jumpstart us now and then. Who knew that the frustration of a house full of new cabinets with no one to hang them would lead to such a satisfying array of productive outcomes? Thank you, Enrique.

4 ⚇ Expect the Unexpected

Bandits Not Invited—Never Know What to Expect in Real Estate

Sam and I entered the rental market for the first time after attempting to sell our 900-square-foot condo on Easy Street in Mountain View, California. Despite the name, our second-story corner unit was not so easy to unload when we wanted to buy a home. We leased it for five years, until the market recovered.

A worrywart at the time, I could not resist taking a peek inside during our Open House. This was my chance to explore the booming potential of Silicon Valley real estate sales in the year 2000.

"What could go wrong?" my even-keel husband asked, "Isn't it a seller's market?"

"Yes," I agreed, "We're the lowest-priced listing in town! And there is only one other condo under $300,000."

I preferred showing it with the tenant's stylish furniture inside but Shelly began to resent the intrusion. I agreed to host the next Open House after she moved out, which she promised to do immediately.

Her door remained locked for two weeks as eager buyers peered through windows or perused the flyer posted on the door.

Shelly finally started packing the eve of the Open House.

I came by to monitor her progress. "Do you need any help?" I tactfully asked as she puttered about.

"Could you help pack the last few boxes and take them to my friend's house?" Shelly replied. I scurried after her, stuffing boxes until midnight, then hurried back to scrub the toilet, clean the fridge, and vacuum the carpets.

Early the next morning I hauled in a few furniture pieces and paintings to define space and add a splash of color. I baked cookies and set flowers in strategic locations. To brighten the dark living room I turned on every light, and to cool down the air I propped the balcony door open. A bubbling water fountain and a row of redwood trees helped drown out the nearby freeway noise. All that the realtor had to do was show up and turn the key.

Sam took the boys for a picnic lunch in a neighborhood park and I headed to our abode.

I noted two police cars parked nearby and muttered, "That's a little disturbing."

Our realtor sign was obscured behind a wall of black and white metal. The big event was scheduled to begin in five minutes.

"Everything is under control," I informed Sam by phone, as I dashed down the street to check out the competing listing. Crossing the threshold, I brushed shoulders with hoards of browsers and elbowed my way to the brochure table.

"We have several people interested in making an offer," the agent said brightly, handing out another glossy flyer.

What our unit lacked in style, this one made up for in abundance. It boasted vaulted ceilings, custom paint colors, and a master bedroom seductively adorned with scented candles. Worse, it offered a master bathroom, which our condo lacked. Views of mature trees and a community pool beckoned out the window. Birds chirped happily and children played. I checked the price. It was the same as ours.

It's all good, I reassured myself, recalling the dearth of homes available for sale. I hustled back to our bare-bones condo to see if the realtor had arrived.

I meant to inquire about the police cars parked outside our complex, but my eyes wandered to the wad of toilet paper stuck to the realtor's chin.

"A shaving accident—I didn't want to spill blood on my white shirt," he explained.

"Just don't forget to remove it," I suggested and shuttled back to join my family for lunch at the park.

A stained shirt turned out to be the least of my worries.

I wolfed down a sandwich and drove by to steal another glance at our Open House. To my alarm, I discovered that nearly a dozen emergency vehicles had joined the police cruisers, including a police van and a police motorcycle.

I stared open-jawed as the row of black and white vehicles trailed around the curb framing our complex. Did I mention the SWAT team and the police helicopter?

"Wha...what is happening over there?" I stuttered as a sweating biker rolled off the trail.

"They're searching for an armed bank robber," he panted.

"In the middle of our Open House? They can't do that!" I insisted.

"Sorry, you won't be selling your place today," he called out as he cycled off to calmer grounds.

Initially, the armed robbery suspect had sought refuge at the popular Shoreline movie theater complex nearby. He fled there after failing to rob a Brink's money truck. (Why do all crooks possess the flight instinct of a squirrel and the brain of a walnut?) He was no better at hiding than he was at stealing: an usher discovered his refuge when patrons complained of bumps nudging along the screen. From the theater, he'd hopped on his motorcycle and high-tailed it to the nature trail. This led him straight down the path to our Open House.

I had prepared a booklet touting the virtues of the area. It was propped open to my favorite feature: the nature trail. Along with "biking, walking, and rollerblading," I never imagined "evading police" as a potential recreational activity. It must have been another slow day in the valley, as officers from every station within a thirty-mile radius descended on our quiet little complex. By the time our Open House ended, the last of the emergency vehicles was trailing off in a cloud of exhaust fumes.

Despite my worst fears, our humble pad sold for $16,000 over asking price—more than any previously marketed condo in that complex. The unexpected turn of events showed me that worrying is pointless and that God has a sense of humor.

How Grass Grows Greener—What Happens When the Slope Isn't Right

Upon selling our condo we chose to upgrade our investment rental to a four-bedroom home in San Diego, in hopes of eventually retiring there. Sam sent me off to Southern California to locate our dream property.

The one-story ranch home on a wooded easement a mile from the beach first grabbed my attention because of the backyard. It wasn't just a lawn; it was a park. Our realtors admired it too and never tired of pointing out how spacious the lawn was. They never noticed—or thought to mention—how the lawn sloped ever so gradually toward the house. Though it resembled more of a dog park with barely a green blade of grass remaining, I dreamed of transforming it into an oasis like the lawns I had envied in my neighborhood. (I forgot about the hours my neighbors spent admiring each new blade of grass as it sprouted, like first-time parents.)

"We'll slap new sod on it," I told Sam. "It will be good as new."

I found a gardener who spoke English; and he immediately set to pulling up the lawn, installing sprinklers and rolling new strips of grass. We enjoyed several years of calm. Our tenants were friendly and paid their rent right on time. They even offered to pay for minor improvements. The house continued to gain in value. We found a new tenant with minimal effort when the first family moved to Canada. I wondered why everyone stressed so much about owning a rental home.

One drizzly day I was watching Nico's soccer game. He was about to score when my cell phone rang. I hovered under a tree to take the call. It was my new tenant, alerting me: "I discovered a little problem with the house."

My heart rate soared. This sounded expensive already. "Tell me more," I prompted between clenched teeth.

"The streets flooded last month after a few days of heavy rain," Dana reported. "I drove through the water to reach Home Depot and bought two dozen forty-pound sand bags, which I threw in front of the garage door and the patio to keep the water from flowing in."

I wondered why she failed to mention this little tidbit months earlier. Assuming she had thwarted a disaster of Biblical proportions, Dana no doubt sighed in relief and went on her merry way. All was fine until she had the impulse to rearrange her family room and discovered incriminating dark spots lining the carpet and the furniture. Was it a mildew colony and did it have relatives anywhere else in the house? (It did, underneath the box spring in her daughter's bedroom. The box spring sat directly on the floor since her daughter was afraid of monsters under the bed.) Dana quickly summoned a friend who had recently endured months of flood repairs and mold remediation. No word evokes more fear and potential fraud than the word MOLD.

Like a pair of detectives, she and her friend tore up every corner of carpet in search of spores. Not a room was spared. As intrepid as the Nile explorers, they forged on, determined to find the source of the moisture.

Suspecting a drainage problem, I called a professional landscaper and his contractor buddy.

"The needle on your outdoor water meter is spinning all over the place; it's a pipe leak," they reported confidently.

I called the leak detection experts. "Good news—you don't have a leak after all." (Now we could celebrate the fact that insurance would not cover this.)

Evidently the water had steadily seeped through our lovely expanse of sod, down the patio, and into the walls. I sprung into action before our house turned into a setting for a horror flick. Who thinks of 100-year rains and flood insurance in a desert climate? It was time to bring in the mold remediation experts.

I carefully investigated contractor licenses and liability coverage. I found one contractor to do all the work since he was the only person who would offer a straight answer about costs. (One firm quoted thousands of dollars to drill inside the drywall for air-quality samples, and suggested hiring a hydraulic engineer to obtain concrete core samples from the patio.)

Our property soon evolved into a biohazard site as masked men in space suits arrived to cover the house in plastic sheets. Quarantine notices warned potential visitors of the hazards lurking inside. I could only imagine the neighbor's tongues wagging as they pictured a murder in the nice, quiet house next door. "But the tenant seemed like such a sweet person," they were thinking. (She really *was*.)

The only crime being committed was the assault on our bank account, yet the long-distance project was progressing in clockwork fashion.

One issue remained—changing the slope of the lawn to avoid future floods.

Bulldozers and bobcats rolled in daily. Updates and photos of the project were e-mailed regularly to assure us that this was actually our house. Fences were thrown aside, sod ripped out, soil stripped bare, and sprinkler systems removed.

The backyard now sat a foot lower. "You won't recognize the place," the contractor informed me while we were vacationing in Maine. "Your house went from being at the bottom of a hill to the top of an island."

In lieu of going green with the eco-friendly measures we had taken at home, we took the "easy" route for our rental and chose to cover the lawn with sod again. Convinced my gardener's quote to lay sod and install new sprinklers was too high, the contractor offered to save us buckets of cash by handling the work himself.

"It's not rocket science," he assured me. "My plumbers have laid sod before and they're good with pipes."

Pleased with the rest of the project, we took the bait. We sent our gardener, Thanh, over to check the progress. We learned several Vietnamese expletives that day, heard half a state away.

Convinced that Thanh was retaliating for not getting the landscaping job, the contractor pushed his concerns aside and accused him of sabotage.

"There is a dent the size of his foot in the sprinkler box and now it doesn't work properly," he alerted us.

"What about the placement of the drainage ditches?" I asked him.

"My workers were just playing a joke on me; they were going to move the ditches back to the right place."

The gurgling water spewing forth from a soggy patch of grass was "normal," the contractor explained, and the brown wasteland along the side of the yard would soon spring back to life. It would just take a few more sprinkler heads; he had purchased the others secondhand from a woman harboring a grudge against her landscaper ex-husband. It seemed *everyone* had a grudge.

I solicited second and third opinions. I attempted to receive the sacred document declaring our home free of mold, which was required for resale purposes; our contractor continued to hold it as leverage.

By now the lawn was seeing more action than an NFL game. Everyone else was afraid to deliver the prognosis until Victor, the lawn doctor, came to the rescue.

"I can fix the grass to make pretty again," he calmly announced, as if consulting on a facial reconstruction. He recommended a complete overhaul and somehow repaired the lawn to pre-flood condition. What a miracle worker he was. He transformed a patchwork quilt of dead grass and spewing geysers into a tapestry of green. The pipes and faulty sprinkler heads were replaced and the sod was stitched back together again. Ditches and drains were strategically relocated.

One builder's failure to grade the lot properly at time of construction cost us $35,000. Yet there were unexpected blessings. Our contractor completed the mold remediation work quickly, so we were able to lease out the home again within a short time frame. He added creative touches like a berm and a retaining wall from recycled pavers. With the help of a wonderful agent we sold our rental investment at the peak of the market—to a lovely family from Scotland who was accustomed to damp conditions. They LOVED the lawn, or as they called it, "the garden."

Despite what was lost, we still came out ahead. We avoided the stress of burning embers from the San Diego fires of 2007 and the real estate market crash of 2008. Still, the next time you wonder how much lawn care might cost, first check the slope. Or your lawn may have you seeing green in more ways than one. Let the plumbers fiddle with the toilet and not with the sprinklers. And when someone offers to save you a ton of money, run the other way as fast as you can!

A Cure for Lead Foot—Beware of Who Is Hiding in the Bushes

Do you suffer from lead-foot syndrome, dashing from one crisis to the next? Does all the busyness leave you too bleary-eyed to notice the speedometer? Let the following tale encourage you to ease off the pedal, should you ever run into George. I failed to notice a motorcycle cop hiding in the bushes two streets from home and now I had to pay my dues.

My usual radar detectors, the kids, were not in the car but that spared me the humiliation of being busted in front of them. The punishment was traffic school; I would try and make the most of it.

I walked into the sweltering classroom one balmy Saturday afternoon and was greeted by a geriatric with a wavy long hairdo and white beard to match. His pants were held up by a pair of red suspenders due to a recent loss of forty pounds, but his belly spilled over the top of his pants. The straps stayed in place, preventing us any comic relief. No doubt he failed all the past *Bad Santa* auditions and was now reduced to teaching traffic school. Judging from the litany of rules and instructions he barked at the class, he would have made a good drill sergeant. I half-expected him to demand laps around the building or push-ups for each infraction.

During the course of that day I was chastised three times—for talking to my neighbor, for digging through my purse, and for glancing at the course booklet. We were allowed to peruse the book only twice, once to take a test and once to look at the drinking and driving statistics.

He nearly drove me to drink! There was no note taking allowed, nor doodling. I was too paranoid to pick up my pen. A Russian man was chastised for leaving his cell phone on. He claimed he did not understand English, but later scored 19/21 on his written test. An Asian woman was berated for looking at her booklet, and another person was reprimanded for dozing off (she pretended to fake an eye injury). The class would have been a good cure for insomnia, had sleeping actually been permitted.

We were expected to remain spellbound at all times. If not, it was quickly brought to our attention and to that of everyone else in the class. When someone was reprimanded, no one quite knew which one of us he was talking to (but having naturally guilty consciences, my neighbor and I assumed it was one of us). You know you're desperate for a diversion when you start reading ingredients on your water bottle.

As if the fear of being called out for talking or reading weren't bad enough, I urgently had to use the facilities. Since sadistic George was on a power kick, I assumed he would decline my request when I asked to be excused for a moment.

"If you have to use the bathroom, it's down the hall," he bellowed. "And do you have a cell phone?" he added accusingly. Who did he expect me to call: 911 for a boredom emergency?

I bolted from the classroom and could not find a women's restroom if my life depended on it. This was the most useful fact he could have passed on. I eyed the bushes longingly but salvaged my dignity and entered the girls' locker room instead. George stepped out of class to ensure I would return. Walking to my little desk at the back of the class required sucking in my gut and doing a side-shuffle down the sliver of remaining aisle where I hoped, in vain, to escape his fanatic attention. Even during the traffic movies, a blessed relief from his ramblings, I caught him casing me out over the rims of his glasses.

After each break he did a roll call to see who remained and then closed the door to our classroom cell. This was no doubt to keep attendees from being distracted by the beautiful spring day that taunted us outside. Each time he offered a few minutes of freedom, he reminded us of the "nice side of George" followed by a stiff warning to return at the appointed time. After one delinquent soul was given the evil eye, there were no more offenders.

I rushed home for lunch, extra cautious to keep one eye on the speed limit and another on the clock. Returning, I squeezed back into my tiny desk to resume the torture. George began his next round of topics in similarly nauseating detail until I wanted to plead for mercy. By mid-afternoon my restless spirit was ready to catapult me from the chair but somehow I remained in place. Ironically, George enjoyed "teaching" as it gave him a chance to "interact with the public" more than his technical writing career allowed. We were given no opportunity to talk; we could not even tell where we had committed our offenses. That would have been helpful, to note what roads to avoid. So much attention was spent on George's old flying days, I wondered if I was in flight school or traffic school. If I ever pursue my pilot's license, at least I will know whose class *not* to take.

At least this mind-numbing experience cured me of my driving transgressions. Should I ever lapse in the future, I may opt to have my insurance raised by hundreds of dollars so the pain will be less drawn-out.

As you dash about town above the speed limit or drive through that orange light, or do a rolling stop, remember George. Then ask yourself "Is it really worth a day in boot camp?"

Can You Hear Me Now?—The "Convenience" of Cell Phones

There is one transgression I will rarely commit while on the road: talking and driving. Talking on the phone is a favorite pastime and I prefer doing it in the comfort of my home. My family says it's good that I am not allergic to plastic since I frequently have a phone plastered to my ear.

Sam's favorite story from when we were dating was when our connection died in mid-call.

"I couldn't get through for an hour as the line was still busy," he said.

Each time Sam tells the story the length of the busy signal gets longer.

It is amazing that we survived a long-distance relationship. He has resisted answering the phone since his childhood days in Korea, when he could never decipher the rapid dialect of the locals who called. He occasionally overcomes this phobia by inventing languages and imaginary characters for the telemarketers who call. After some nonsense gibberish, he will switch to another voice, "I'm sorry my father doesn't understand English. Let me translate for you. He thinks you have insulted his honor…"

My twin sister Hett and I do not share this phone fetish. AT&T should have a calling plan named in honor of us since we provide them so much business. But like a binge eater, I prefer to talk behind closed doors. This also prevents callers from hearing the alarming sounds of fighting children. With the advent of cell phones, we have now become part of everyone's conversation. One never knows what drama to expect; at times, it is tempting to join in.

"He's doing what? She is dating *which* guy? Do tell!" Who needs Ann Landers anymore? Just describe your dilemma in public and see who jumps in with advice. Granted, certain professions merit the need to be "on call." However, must people start talking in the middle of a church service or a $10 movie? It's like the rest of the population is invisible at the first ring.Convenience takes precedence over consideration. There is no need to converse in person anymore since someone more important beckons a few wavelengths away.

At any given moment, one can enter a crowded intersection and see a cell phone attached to an ear at every corner. I can never say hello to people anymore because they are always talking to someone else. The true veterans don't bother with the hassle of holding up a phone; they simply keep a microphone curled behind their ear. This look used to be reserved for the Secret Service. Then there are those who wear their phones around their neck like a fashion accessory, or hanging on their belt with other handy gadgets. The phone acts as a camera, organizer, GPS unit, and minicomputer. It's become the portable office in a pocket.

I never know how people can get a signal all the time. How is it that people are connecting on Mount Everest, and I can't get reception from the frozen food aisle? I feel like the commercial, "Can you hear me now? Can you hear me now?" Is my monthly fee really worth it so I can check whether we need peas or corn, or which movie my family wants to watch? Despite the comfort of feeling connected, I don't always want everyone to find me wherever I am, like the woman I overheard answering her cell phone by saying, "How did you know I was here?"

When I first obtained a cell phone, I felt I had to keep talking to get my money's worth so I temporarily downgraded from the "all you can talk plan" to the diet version of "pay as you go." This also lowered the financial risk of losing the phone.

Before growing accustomed to my cell phone, I should have been required to have a license to use it. Sam never knew what to expect when attempting to call me. I either had it turned off, buried in my pants pocket, or I neglected to charge the battery. My choir partner, Joan, has managed to keep the same pencil in her music folder for twenty years, whereas I do well to remember to return the cell phone to my purse.

When the kids were little I called our babysitter to say we were running late for a date. Sam parked the car outside her house while I set my phone down on a flat surface, unbuckled Nico from his infant car seat, and helped Kyle out of his booster seat. Loaded down like a Sherpa, I deposited kids and gear inside. Then we dashed off to the movie theater to catch the start of *Saving Private Ryan* before we missed all of D-Day.

It wasn't until later that evening that I noticed the deflated side pocket of my purse.

"Did the phone fall out of your pants in the toilet stall at the theater?" my helpful husband inquired.

"Retrace your steps" is Sam's mantra.

Did I drop it in the Safeway parking lot that morning, like I had with his keys once? (While searching for those I lost the library videos that flew off the top of the car—now I leave multitasking to my teenager.)

I jiggled my brain to imagine what forlorn spot my cell phone lay in as I tried calling it.

Had the phone retained any spark of life, it might have attempted a ring. But this poor hunk of plastic had never even reached the movie theater; it spent the night in front of the babysitter's house. When I visited the scene the next morning, I discovered a trail of black shards splattered up and down the street. Upon closer examination, I saw the word *Nokia* on one piece and the flattened remnants of a computer chip nearby. I returned home to dispose of the remains. There was nothing left to recycle.

As Nico grew older, he became the "secretary" who always knows where everything is. "Have you seen the battery recharger?" I could ask and he'd fire back: "Kitchen, far right side, top drawer, next to the tape measure." I wondered if he started hiding things on purpose after I made the mistake of offering finder fees. He had his eye on a new Lego set and we had already purchased all the ten-dollar sets.

I now remember to keep the phone and recharger in the same place, to charge it regularly, and to keep it turned on. This came in handy when the phone fell on the curb in front of the neighbors' house. I have no idea how it wandered there, but imagine my surprise when I stepped outside and it started to ring. For once it was not me calling the phone. It was Kyle ringing me from the bathroom to inform me he was out of toilet paper.

These days, people take and make calls from anywhere, at all times. If the cashier has not been replaced by an automated self-checker that lectures you about unclaimed items in the bagging area, then shoppers talk during their transaction as if everyone else is irrelevant.

Technological gadgets both help and hinder us. They can cause us to miss what is right in front of us. I dream of a time when we will talk to each other in person. I dream of a time when conversations do not end abruptly in mid-sentence. I dream of a place where we always have reception. Maybe that is too much to expect. Can you hear me now?

Need a Boost?—A Little Help from a Stranger

Like many ambitious moms, I often combine multiple stops in one outing. On my way home from a Bible study class once, I set out to deliver a gift to a new mom with twins. I turned the key in the ignition. Not a sputter of life. I tried again…still nothing. Not wanting to waste a cell call to AAA for something so easily remedied, I dashed inside the church to see if anyone had jumper cables.

One of the childcare workers volunteered her spouse's services. "He likes helping people," she said. Perfect!

True to her word, he strolled over with cables in hand. The car sprang to action at the first turn of the key and I confidently drove off. Spotting a Wells Fargo bank on the way, I remembered I needed cash, so I pulled into a spot next to the ATM machine. Just as my car battery ground to a halt, the battery on my cell phone died also. Perhaps they were in cahoots. A young woman in business attire handed me her phone, but still I hesitated to summon AAA in case I needed to call for a more pressing problem down the road.

Spying an industrious-looking gardener, I called out casually, "Do you have jumper cables?"

"Yes Missus," he replied enthusiastically, as he made a U-turn toward the bank parking lot and pulled his car up in front of mine. I grimaced as cars whizzed by, not wanting him to grace the cover of the next day's newspaper: *Gardener Flattened While Helping Cheapskate Motorist*. After rummaging in the cab of his truck, he discovered that his jumper cables were not there after all.

Not easily discouraged, he fashioned a set of cables out of a piece of wire and some pliers. Nice, cute, handy, and helpful, all at the same time; I like that in a man.

With the first few attempts a spark flickered, then petered out. At this point I started fishing out my auto rescue card.

"Let me try one more time," he insisted. Pressing the wires down with his bare hands, I watched to see if his fingers would start sizzling. Now I was begging him to let me call AAA.

"I have done this once before and it worked," he continued intently, poking at a few more wires.

I held my breath.

As if on cue, the engine roared to life. With a beaming smile he walked away, turning down my offer for a free lunch.

Maybe next time I will try roadside assistance, but I doubt it will be as much fun.

I am still waiting for AAA to offer boat service. Until then, I will rely on the continued kindness of strangers and the lake patrol....

A few months after the stalled battery incident, I decided a boat outing would be the perfect way to end the summer. I pulled some picnic supplies together and lured the boys away from their technology toys. After a sixty-minute drive through the golden, grapevine-studded hills of Livermore, California, we arrived at Lake Del Valle. Ferrying away from the dock, the sparkling clear waters beckoned me and I convinced Sam to stop the boat for a quick swim.

I paddled around in the water then clambered back on board. After cutting the engine my determined husband, try as he might, could not get our fine rental craft started again. A family coasted up to us as

Sam stood sweating in the hot sun, yanking on the motor's starter cord. Still no hint of life sounded.

I eyed their motor longingly. Our boat was due back in forty minutes; I quickly calculated how long it would take us to row back to avoid a search party or lose our $50 deposit. Alas, I did not need to beg for assistance. The motorboat, stuffed to the brim with five adults and a child, chugged up behind us.

"Need a tow?" the man called out cheerfully across the water.

Drawing on his Boy Scout training, Sam quickly crafted a figure-eight knot and attached us to the end of their boat. We could barely manage to keep from knocking into their stern as we limped along in a trail of exhaust fumes, at the mercy of their overtaxed motor.

Soon the motor of our good Samaritans started choking and sputtering until there was nothing but the sound of the water lapping against our two boats. Efforts to revive the motor by dousing it with water were met with more hissing and smoke. After pulling the top off and inspecting its innards, the skipper discovered a hose had broken. Just when he wondered what to do next, the motor coughed back to life at half its former luster.

With apologies and well wishes, the family untied us from their rope and headed back to the dock, promising to alert the rental office of our predicament. As their Middle Eastern pop tunes faded from earshot, we heard the hopeful sound of the lake patrol. True to their word, help arrived and we were towed to shore.

A temporary frustration turned into more memories and a free coupon for a future boat rental. We managed to ignite our portable barbecue without setting the drought-stricken landscape ablaze and we enjoyed a meal of burgers and apple pie. The boys had fun fishing and skipping rocks in the water and we were treated to a bald eagle soaring overhead. Even with a few minor setbacks like dying boats, a burger dropping into the ashes, and forgotten bathing suits, we deemed the outing a success. The glow of the golden hills over the water provided a stunning backdrop for our evening picnic.

Once we revise our idea of success, any outing can be salvaged. In the future, if you see a stalled vehicle please toss out a rope. It may be us.

Come Back Soon—Why Two Works Better Than One

Sometimes I need to be gone for a few days to realize how much Sam does to help keep the family afloat, even if the evidence is not always obvious upon return. Typically I attempt one last effort to restore order before my departure, but time inevitably runs out before the dash to the airport. When I walk back into the house, days later, every item is in an arrested state of preservation. The broom is still propped against the wall like a sentry dozing at his post.

On one trip I came home to find supper leftovers that I had forgotten to toss; it was left growing on the stove for a future science experiment. I pulled off the lid and discovered three varieties of mold.

"Are you creating a new brand of penicillin for your next science fair project?" I asked the kids.

Now when I return and express disappointment that order has not been magically restored in my absence, Sam reminds me that I am holding him to the high standards of a hotel room with daily cleaning service, or a perpetually neat family member. Instead of griping, I am grateful that he graciously volunteers an occasional weekend of childcare so that I can enjoy time away. How do single parents ever get a break? I try to remain thankful when the toilet papers holders are empty, the laundry baskets are spilling over, and the new shampoo bottle is emptied after one shower. At least the boys have upgraded from baths, a duty I relinquished after the flood. Ignoring my instincts, I once trusted the boys to take a bath together when they were four and eight years old. They insisted that they were perfectly capable of scrubbing themselves without my help.

"It sounds like you're having way too much fun in there," I called through the door.

Sheepishly exiting the bathroom they quickly shut the door to hide the evidence.

I turned the doorknob. It was locked tight. *No problem, I have a little gizmo to open it.*

I reached on top of the doorframe where we normally kept it. I rummaged through the junk drawer and the toolbox. I tried substitutes. Still unable to pop the lock from the outside, I waited till morning to call Sam, who was in England on a business trip.

When I finally got in there and surveyed the damage I saw that our vinyl bathroom floor had become a lake bottom and only half the water in the tub remained. First I surmised it had somehow sprung a leak overnight. By morning the water was still seeping through the drywall, staining the hardwood floor on the other side.

Making lemonade from lemons, I seized the opportunity for a bathroom remodel and upgraded the second bathroom at the same time. As an added bonus, Sam offered to handle all bath and bedtime chores thereafter.

Sam always makes it clear that if I want his help I must accept that he will use the system that works best for him. He never deviates from his routines so he knows what to expect. Bedtime routines are casual at best; rather than fight to haul kids off to brush their teeth in front of a sink, Sam used to let them brush their teeth in bed and spit into a cup. For him the bigger victory is in landing them in their beds, not in brushing and flossing for two minutes.

Not getting undressed is another one of Sam's handy time-saving devices. I am no longer surprised to wake up and discover the boys in the same clothes as when they went to bed. One can guess how many days have elapsed by the degree of stains on their shirts. When the original color is no longer discernable, even the kids know it is time to change. The daytime wear doubles as nightclothes.

"Why waste time changing if it means an extra few minutes of sleep in the morning?" my practical husband will ask.

I empathize with the plight of the single-parent household. One night I filled in for Sam's normal garbage duty. *How hard can this be?* I wondered as I brought the recycling, garden waste, and garbage cans out to the curb.

The next morning I rolled the cans back up the driveway. Then it hit me—two weeks earlier I had agreed to take out the neighbors' garbage while they were on vacation. They were coming home to a heat wave the following day and would soon discover my oversight.

Initially I considered the old switcheroo; they would likely never notice the different can. When I discovered the all-too-obvious tear in our lid, I decided the only thing worse than being derelict in my sanitation duties would be to take the neighbors' receptacle and replace it with a defective one. The least incriminating option would be to retrieve the neighbors' bag and add it to our empty can. I ran toward their house as the unseasonably warm sun beat upon my neck. Just as I wondered about the effects of waste products baking in steaming confines after a heat wave, I noticed the maggots inching their way down the garbage bin. I hosed the culprits towards a bush at the end of the driveway in hopes they would slide down the sewer before the neighbors returned.

When they later thanked me for taking out their garbage, I smiled innocently while making a mental note to record such details on my calendar next time.

When Sam is straddled with responsibilities both at work and at home, another small duty I have offered to take on is the barbecuing. Grilled meat always smells so good—when other people are cooking it.

I used to toss a few pieces of meat on the rack and go back inside to do something else, until my kids would ask, at the first sign of billowing smoke, "Shouldn't you check on the grill?"

I now monitor the grill closely to prevent the burgers from evolving into unrecognizable lumps of charcoal that even our dog shuns. It would be handy to have a paging device like some restaurants offer: "Your burgers are ready. Please return to the barbecue area."

The other crucial skill I have learned from Sam is time management. I sometimes harbor overly ambitious expectations of how much activity can be squeezed into sixty minutes. My ever-punctual partner will have all his activities generously spaced apart and programmed in his computer's "To Do" list, with a reminder chiming at the appointed hour. Another mantra of my dependable husband is, "Sometimes being on time means having to be early."

I was quite proud to be early and the first to arrive for a PTA board dinner meeting. When no one else arrived within the next ten minutes, my pride turned to concern. Then I pulled the Day Planner from my purse to check the time: I had the right time, just the wrong restaurant.

There is so much that I take for granted sometimes, like a husband who is always at the right place at the right time and who comes home at a reasonable hour every night. When I dread awaking to buzzers, Sam acts as my alarm clock and willingly drives me to the airport for 6:00AM flights. He is not afraid of dirty jobs; he will clean spills, plunge toilets, and squash computer bugs and other critters. Sam is the one who keeps us ticking. Instead of dwelling on tasks he opts not to do, I am thankful for his many contributions that make our lives easier. Except on school Pajama Days—our kids are the only ones who have to change out of their clothes and into PJs in the morning.

I Like the Red One—Fighting Off Feisty Car Salesmen

Spontaneity is an admirable quality but there are times when impulses should be ignored.

Sam has always lusted for a convertible. (This love of the open air was perhaps inspired by their parents who began their married life touring Europe on a Moped.) Sam's first convertible was a Suzuki Samurai which was a rattlebox on wheels, but he liked the way the wind whipped his wavy hair back and women admired him at the stoplights.

One day as I was driving home from an errand, I could not resist the urge to stop by a Toyota used-car lot where I spotted a red Celica convertible glistening in the sun.

What a fine birthday present that would make for Sam. He asks for so little: a clear path through the house, a fresh bath towel, and a supply of non-alcoholic beer.

The salesman approached me, pumping his arms like a goose on steroids. Normally intimidated by such a display of aggression, I did not sprint back to the safety of my car. I stood my ground, sat inside the car and admired the slick feel of its smooth leather seats. Then he put the top down and I fell in love.

The salesman seduced me with more features and I did not say "Stop, let's wait!" when he handed me the keys. I agreed to the test drive. He pointed me down several city streets. We drove past the turnoff to our street.

Suddenly I developed the urge to surprise Sam with this sparkling wonder and park it on our driveway. He hates surprises.

The salesman and I drove up stealthily in the gleaming convertible, as subtle as a fire truck. Leaning back in the passenger seat, I felt like a movie star amid such splendor. He demonstrated the ease by which the rooftop magically lifted up from the back trunk area and locked back into place to secure the vehicle. Then I climbed out of the driver's seat, hitting the "lock all doors" button out of habit on my way out.

I instructed the salesman to hide from view behind the overgrown bush towering beside our driveway.

Once the salesman was safely out of sight, I lured Sam out of his office cave. With one eyebrow raised he looked at me and then at the convertible.

"How do you like it?" I asked in my best Vanna White impression. "Look how easily the top opens up!"

I attempted to open the passenger door to activate the switch.

At this moment the salesman popped up from the bush and leaned over the side of the car, peering desperately at his keys dangling from the ignition.

I scurried off to find an implement to pry open the car and our then seven-year-old son Kyle helpfully volunteered his skinny arm. Fortunately one window was slightly ajar so he easily jimmied the door open.

Before causing a further debacle I quickly hopped in, accepting the salesman's brave offer of allowing me to drive again. Sam fired dubious looks in my direction.

Back at the dealership, the salesman let me fondle the key for a while in the hopes I would take this puppy home permanently. Abruptly he was summoned away to a more pressing obligation. Upon returning he asked me for the key, which I assured him was no longer in my possession. He scurried off to search for it. Marveling at my chance to weasel out of a sales pitch, I snuck out the lot. In my foggy allergy state I failed to notice, until emptying my pockets later, that indeed I had the missing car key.

It's a wonder he kept his job. I eventually donated our aging red Mazda to an aspiring sports agent in need of wheels

for work and school, and negotiated a great deal on a Mitsubishi Eclipse convertible from Craigslist.

Years later, driving my kids through the African Lion Safari in Cambridge, Ontario, Kyle and Nico begged me to follow signs to the baboon enclosure, but for once I was leery of taking a risk. We were in a rental car and I didn't know how I would explain large dents in the roof or a missing antenna. I opted for the bypass route and observed from a distance as families of pink-bottomed baboons descended upon the cruising cars. Like a flock of overzealous car salesmen they ambushed the visitors. I plotted out a potential escape route, along the grass, in case we dared to circle back later to join the action.

"What about living on the edge?" the kids challenged me.

And so, after completing one loop of the park, I eased my compact sedan into a row of more tempting alternatives of SUVs with large racks and cargo holds. Trying to remain inconspicuous in our sparkling red rental car, we kept our windows and doors securely shut and our wheels rolling forward. And then we prayed. The baboons completely avoided us. The boys gained the best memory of our whole trip and I earned extra points for coolness. Some risks are worth taking as long as you know there is a way out.

5 ⚡ Take Time To Play

Pick Your Poison—Sometimes It's Safer to Stay on the Boat

There is a nothing like connecting with nature—until you leave the path. "Can't you read the sign?" my law-abiding teenage son Kyle accused as we trudged up a Bay Area trail one summer, as I strayed off to snap a photograph. Kyle believes this propensity to occasionally bend rules is what led to my encounter with a three-lobed plant. ("Leaves of three, let it be," Sam always says.)

Personally I think my fate was sealed during the kayaking outing the next day. Some people prefer dodging crowds at the mall over dealing with the hidden hazards of the outdoors. Then again, what trouble could one attract while seated in a protective bubble of plastic on a beautiful Fourth of July weekend?

The afternoon started out benignly enough. Cruising along the water's edge of the Stephen's Creek Reservoir, I admired the grace of a blue heron as it skimmed the water like a glider coasting in for a landing. A startled egret flew off from a nearby marshy bank. I turned my attention back to paddling. Then I caught a flicker of movement in the water. I peered beneath the surface to see if it was a turtle. The neck of a beer bottle bobbed to the surface. Outraged that someone would desecrate my special getaway, I plucked it out of the water and dropped it into my kayak with a satisfying thump. Soon I found another bottle, and another, and another.... At this rate I would have enough glass to start a recycling plant. I fished out a shoe, its partner long since vanished.

Next, a Styrofoam cooler protruded from the sandy bottom like a long-lost treasure chest waiting to be opened. I chose not to disturb its final resting place and continued to stroke my way past rocky outcrops and knotted oak trees. After combing one side of the lake for more telltale signs of litter, I made a goal to clear the whole circumference of the lake. It had been awhile since I had set any significant goals for myself; if I couldn't cool the global warming crisis, then at least I would leave the environment more pristine. I should have known not to turn playtime into work.

Rounding a bend in the lake, I discovered the mother lode of trash: dozens of discarded fish bait containers lay scattered on the sandy beach. Fishing lures and red bobbers dangled in trees like Christmas ornaments. A tennis ball floated in the water. I pulled the kayak to shore and more treasures greeted me on the bank. The remains of a tattered T-shirt hung in strips, pierced by a bush. Several empty take-out containers littered the ground. Angrily I snatched up one incriminating piece of evidence after another.

Farther and farther up the slope I foraged for loot. Cresting the hill, I spotted a trashcan next to a pullout at the side of the road. I dumped the sordid pile into the can. When the landscape no longer resembled a teen sleepover gone wild, I returned to the kayak where the rest of my trash haul awaited me. Paddling along in ninety-degree weather, I noted several people ignoring the "No Swimming" signs. One young, damp-haired girl glanced toward my unsightly stash, turned to her dad, and said, "Yuck, she's sitting in garbage!" Of course, she had been swimming in garbage moments before.

Upon returning from my ecological expedition, I decided to reward my efforts with a long soak in the tub. Wrinkled skin turned out to be the least of my problems. The next morning I spotted an arc of blisters on my forearm. I examined my bicep and noted a few more red blotches. Like a virus gone rampant, the bumps expanded and multiplied with each itchy day. Despite knowing better, I could not resist scratching. This only caused the rash to spread at a more furious pace. Sam offered his diagnosis: Poison Oak. He is always right about things. Soon I sported red welts on every part of my body. In a desperate attempt to assuage the itching, I wrapped my arm up in an Ace bandage, which only caused the sores to blister more. I felt grateful my face had not yet turned into a grotesque lump, forcing me to hide behind a mask of gauze pads.

I combed the pharmacy aisles for a cure. From calamine lotion to countless poison ivy creams and prescription ointments, I purchased them all. Various online sites offered contradictory homespun treatments: "Try moisturizer; try rubbing your skin in chlorine; take hot showers; take cold showers." By this time I had sampled every soothing skin care product developed within the last century. A prescription cream from the doctor had no effect. As my skin screamed for relief in the night, I returned to the fridge for more ice packs to numb the skin into oblivion.

By day I beached on the bottom of our old kiddy pool, slathered in sunscreen. I washed my sheets and clothing daily to avoid contaminating the rest of the family. They wondered when the wife and mother they used to know would return. To his credit, Sam never once threatened to leave me, despite my pitiful whining.

My trusted allergist came to the rescue, saving us all from further misery. Studying the impressive trail of welts, the doctor reassured me, "I've seen worse," as he tried to keep a straight face. "You're going to have to take your shirt off," he announced casually. Then he turned to me and asked, "Now tell me, did it spread to your crotch?" As I nodded my head, he replied, "I don't need to see it!" Three weeks of prescription skin creams and two rounds of steroid pills later, the rash showed signs of simmering down, and my skin no longer resembled a mutant virus. A week swimming in the salty waters off Catalina Island, near Los Angeles, turned out to be the best cure of all.

Nothing can keep me away from the calming effect of nature. The next time I was exposed to poison oak—and three ticks who hitchhiked to Canada with me—I called my allergist for a stronger prescription. He always puts a smile back on my face (even without the drugs). In future, I will stay in the boat, remain on trails, check for ticks, and wear gloves should the urge to collect trash spontaneously arise. As my good doctor Steve quipped, "So much for altruism!"

The Love Boat—Are Cruises All They're Cracked Up to Be?

The idea of a Caribbean cruise sounded tempting one rainy winter day at home with kids. I nostalgically recalled the romance and frills of *The Love Boat* TV series popular during my college years. Contemplating how to enjoy our tax return, I consulted those who extol the virtues of a vacation at sea. Could this be the antidote to a stressful year?

I reminisced about earlier exploits on the water. Having once hired the low-budget version of an all-day Zodiac boat tour in Hawaii, Sam and I joined a motley crew that included a surfer-type dad, his sidekick fisherman partner, and their hitchhiker friend who we found floating in the water with a garbage bag full of camping gear. The fisherman sat strategically next to the diesel-fumed outboard motor with rod in hand, ready to snag his catch of the day, while nearby passengers turned green in the fifteen-foot waves. After popping a few Tylenols, the skipper offered passengers the opportunity to stop by his house for a portion of the haul that was just reeled in. When we showed up that night to receive our free main course he appeared startled that someone was not too seasick to take him up on it. Sam typically turns his nose up at fish but had never tasted tuna pulled from the ocean an hour before. We fried it in butter and wolfed it down with chunks of garlic and lemon juice that drooled down our chins.

This is my impression of boating trips: there are those who savor fine food and beverages and those who puke them up. I have heard of people spending half their savings for the vacation of a lifetime, and once the cruise ship leaves the dock they can barely stumble from their bunks between the potty runs and the Dramamine refills. Their only view of the sea is a fleeting glimpse out a porthole window.

While I love the water and never get seasick, I wondered if I would have the attention span to make it out of port. Where would I go for an escape? Do people get island fever, or are they too busy bingeing at the buffet table to waddle over to the other side of the boat? My inquisitive spirit always wants to know what lies around the next bend, and what new places and activities await. In researching all the entertainment options aboard a cruise, I imagined spending my whole life aboard a boat. (Then I read of a woman who did just that—it was cheaper than a retirement village.) There would be enough food for years and enough attractions to rival a week at Disneyland. There is rock climbing, swimming, and scuba diving. Science camps are touted as opportunities to learn and socialize at sea.

In order to imagine the plethora of activities available, I consulted a friend who worked for a major cruise line. I needed to dispel the myth that all passengers lounge in the sun sipping umbrella-topped daiquiris recovering from the buffet line. Those who needed to burn off their calories could seek out bronze-muscled trainers and masseuses in the fitness area. For more hands-on activities, there was the miniature skating rink, golf course, and a wave simulator.

For the more thrill-seeking adult crowd, there was poker and bingo, karaoke and talent shows: "Enough options to make anyone indecisive," a popular cruise line promised. "Passengers can recapture their childhood playfulness with recreational thrills such as feeding a shark, kite surfing, and wake boarding," the website read. After swimming over a shark in Hawaii, I learned that I do not need that kind of thrill.

For some, all these diversions would be paradise; for others, the release of tension is more stressful than work. I chatted with a former cruise employee who recalled various Type-A personalities she had served on board. While the ship puttered along the aqua blue waters of the Caribbean, more than one of her passengers' hearts had simply stopped beating! Those they could not revive were stored in a freezer until they returned to shore. One could only hope the assistant chef did not accidentally tug the wrong door open during his daily dinner preparation. Imagine what that would do to his culinary inspiration.

Webster's defines rest as "relief from anything tiring." I worried that all that lounging might be fatiguing in itself. I knew that there were cruises that keep active brains busy and consulted the Web to learn about the offerings of Insight Cruises (formerly geekcruises.com). They advertise "an experience where the right and left side of the brain travel together." You could experience the wonders of the Orient and the fine points of computer programming at the same time.

I quizzed a travel agent friend about her on-shore outings, an important component of cruise trips. Paula cautioned me about the bar-coded passes used to track the passengers as they debarked and re-boarded the ship. Her pass, and that of her son, had become demagnetized once in her wallet. As Paula boarded the ship after a quick jaunt to buy souvenirs, employees instructed her to reactivate the passes immediately. With the next excursion still days away, she opted to take care of it in the morning. She went to freshen up and dress for a dinner party. She and her husband Dan then strolled to the upper deck, leaving their pager in their room.

"Wasn't the boat supposed to leave an hour ago?" Dan asked Paula, as he helped himself to another appetizer. Overhearing their conversation, another passenger informed them that two passengers were missing. Thirty more minutes passed. Twenty-five hundred passengers eagerly anticipated their next heart-stopping adventure, while the boat sat in port waiting for the two stragglers. As the boat finally motored off into the night, Paula fretted over the poor souls who would have to fly to the next stop.

The next morning Dan saw that he had a page. Curiously, he read the message: "Are your wife and son aboard the ship?"

Paula called the crew member back and sheepishly admitted she and her son were safely on board, then hurried off to get a new excursion card.

Next I considered a comedy cruise, based out of the United Kingdom. A research study there revealed that people laugh only six minutes a day—three times less than fifty years ago. When did life become so serious? The good news was that 54 percent of Brits surveyed admitted to laughing more often when on holiday and two thirds more when the sun was shining.

Then, of course, there was the romance cruise to bring the sunshine back into life. My friend Paula advised me against bunking next to a honeymooning couple. To set the mood, her neighboring shipmates had lit candles around their room, leading to sounds of passion bouncing through the walls, along with torrents of water when the sprinklers were set off. For days, the nearby rooms reeked of burnt wicks and musty carpets. The educational cruise might be safer. Hopefully we would avoid an *E. coli* outbreak among a boat full of technology nerds.

How would we ever choose? As the Royal Caribbean website promised, all these options did put me in a quandary. With the current economy, perhaps we should stay at home? A fellow California transplant reminded me that sometimes the best things in life are found in our own backyards. In the end I decided to stick an umbrella in my drink and lounge next to our inflatable pool while Sam bellowed out karaoke tunes in the distance.

Should Have Been Here Earlier—For Those with Bad Timing

Do you ever feel like a jinx when it comes to timing your holiday getaway? No matter how perfect the weather has been, lightning strikes the minute you arrive? If an area has experienced a seven-year drought, a torrential downpour will hit just as you enter the city limit.

San Diego offers stunning two-person kayaking tours in a protected bay. At least that is what the brochures showed. My friend Caryl and I looked forward to a serene outing away from our kids. First we celebrated with one of Caryl's tasty gourmet lunches, and then cut across the coastal hills towards the trendy town of La Jolla. Along the way we gorged on fresh-picked strawberries. Upon reaching the kayak rental store, we suited up and received our launching instructions from the guide. "It's been as smooth as glass all week, like a lake." These were her exact words.

The second we approached the beach, the water evolved into giant swells. Wanting to get the launch over with as quickly as possible, Caryl volunteered us to go first. We waited for the guide to muscle fellow kayakers through the surf, perched in our tandem kayak like drunken ducks. Out of nowhere a large wave rolled into shore, flipping our vessel onto its side. The paddle I was gripping only seconds before landed on her salt-soaked head. Before we knew what hit us, we were swallowing seawater and lunging for gear. We clambered back on board.

All this churning had an adverse effect on Caryl's stomach. "Are you sure you're okay?" I asked as her face turned a deeper shade of green. "Do you want me to sit in back?" I asked, but she bravely resumed her steering and surged on.

By the time we reached the caves the brochures had idyllically suggested swimming in, the surf was crashing into the cliffs, dashing any hopes of entering. We headed for the kelp forest beds where harbor seals snacked on a late lunch. They heard Caryl say, "I think I'm going to…" and darted over, quickly abandoning their dull daily fare as my friend upchucked a smorgasbord of crab salad and chocolate mousse pie. I quickly paddled us away so as not to gross out everyone else on the tour.

When Sam once had to back out of a white-water rafting trip to finish writing a research paper, my brave friend Rachel offered to buy the ticket. Judging from experience, I knew any outing with Rachel would turn into an adventure.

We awoke early and drove several hours to the designated launching site on the American River outside of Sacramento. As we absorbed the instructions of our macho guide, Max, I asked him about helmets. "You don't have to wear them. This is only a Class 2 river, great for beginners," he assured us.

Max loaded the rafts into the water and Rachel gingerly stepped in. The river was low after a lengthy drought, but no problem. "The water was released from the dam into the river this morning," our fearless leader pumped. "It will be awesome!" Within minutes of shoving off from the bank we bounced off boulder after boulder like bumper cars. "The water is never like this," he said, shaking his head in wonder. "They must have stopped letting out water a little too early today."

Turned out, the guide and I were the only ones not ejected into the alpine water. While the others bobbed up and down, I scanned the horizon desperately for a glimpse of Rachel. (She never thought to inform me until moments before that she had never learned how to swim, despite having a father who was a lifeguard.) A splash of red jacket appeared for a second, only to submerge again. I kept my eyes glued to the surf.

Her soggy seatmates plucked her out the water a mile downriver, after she managed to surge through every rapid. What water remained in the river came spilling into our boat, as Rachel heaved once more. We quickly pulled up to shore to seek help before hypothermia set in.

Undaunted, Rachel started planning her next rafting trip within several months. Thankfully, she did not invite me along.

When Sam and I took the kids on a whale-watching adventure years later we passed on the Zodiac raft tour in lieu of the more seaworthy catamaran. As we motored away from the New Brunswick coastline I wondered if we had picked the right leader. Several whales had just been spotted offshore. Excitement filled the air as passengers jostled for position. We leaned into the wind and the salty spray of the ocean as the boat zoomed over to the alleged site. While smaller boats parked at the scene of the presumed action, our eco-sensitive captain chose to wait patiently in the distance and wait for the graceful mammals to glide over to us.

"They will swim here within minutes," he reported confidently.

We waited.

"They never stay under water so long," he continued. "This area is usually teeming with herring—the whales love to feed on them."

A fellow passenger regaled me with tales of his previous Bay of Fundy trip where he was splashed by breeching whales surfacing alongside the boat. I listened to play-by-play details of the hundred close-ups he had taken of the giant pod gliding by. I patted my camera in anticipation.

"Pay attention: Keep watching the horizon," the captain commanded. "There's a spout!" he shouted. I peered into the sea, brimming with optimism.

Oops, too late.

This wasn't supposed to be work; it was summer vacation. And wasn't it his job to find the whales? Crackling reports of sightings sputtered from the radio. My eyes vainly scanned the expanse of sea, bringing to mind my shooting star experiences.

"There, another spout!"

Darn, missed it again.

After two hours the boats finally chugged in a lazy half-circle back towards the dock. Just then the sliver of a whale's back surfaced in the distance, leaving a trail of white froth.

If only we had been there earlier!

This was much like the 1000-mile weekend drive I talked Sam into. We were planning to behold the beauty of desert wildflowers in Southern California. After a record El Niño rain season, naturalists had predicted a record number of wildflowers. Some had been dormant for years. I couldn't miss this spectacle of nature, especially since I had just bought a new Canon camera with a great zoom lens that I was itching to try out. Photographing flowers is my passion.

"We'll have a good blooming year, which happens only a couple of times a decade," a State Park employee promised. Past profusions of flowers included the Desert Sunflower, the elusive Desert Five-Spot, and the "Holy Grail" of desert wildflowers: the Desert Lily. Flowers with intriguing names like Gravel Ghost and the Brown-Eyed Primrose were also expected, along with brilliant red Ocotillo plants and fields of yellow and white annuals.

The perfect combination of timing and weather would determine which specimens bloomed and remained visible for all to see before succumbing to the hot sun and desert caterpillars. Rain followed by wind could dry out the soil, resulting in a poor yield, but rain followed by warm weather could make flowers "pop."

We had a two-day weekend to catch the peak. The flowers chose Monday to burst into bloom. You might want to consult with me before you schedule your next outing. Then pick another time.

Can Everything Go Right?—Taking a Risk with Holiday Travel

Being a substitute teacher has taught me to minimize risk. But sometimes you just have to go for it. A man once told me, "We are always fifteen minutes away from disaster." With that kind of outlook, I'm surprised he dares to walk out the door in the morning.

Do you have days that droop from the start and deteriorate from there; or days when everything you touch is golden? Life is a garden of rosy and thorny moments. The key is to not be so fearful of decisions that all joy is lost. Because the only thing worse than wondering "What-if" is "If only." Rather than worry about getting snagged, I have learned to take more chances. The results can be surprising.

I had planned a quiet Christmas at home in 2008. Why travel during peak season unless absolutely necessary? I might get trapped in the terminal. Or catch a nasty virus on the plane. Rather than a quick jaunt to see my twin, the simple thing would be to stay at home. I had already seen her three times in the last eight months, a record for us. Still, I could not ignore the voice that told me to help make her first Christmas on the West Coast a special one. I watched the fares wax and wane and booked a ticket online, selecting early flights and quieter travel days.

Two weeks later I arrived at the San Francisco airport, with plenty of time to spare before departure. So much time, in fact, that United Airlines' partner airline offered me a seat on an earlier flight—a roomy bulkhead seat! The Air Canada plane had movie players at every seat offering comedies that were actually funny. Drinks were served on the plane; I received the whole can and did not have to pay for it.

After landing bleary-eyed at Vancouver International Airport, I approached customs. Sam had warned me how busy this airport could be. Every booth was barren. I breezed through and went up the escalator to page Hett, since she was not expecting me for another hour. As the escalator propelled me to the upper floor, a woman in a turquoise ski jacket heading down the stairs turned towards me. Happily, I saw that it was Hett. She and her husband Mark completed their descent and hurried back up to greet me. After a ninety-minute ferry ride from Victoria and two bus transfers to Vancouver airport, who would have expected us to arrive at the same spot at the same time?

Mark predicted catching the next ferry was too much to hope for on top of that, so naturally that made Hett and me determined to try. Mark proved right but we remained in high spirits and took advantage of the food court at the ferry terminal. In a classic twin moment we both ordered the same type of salad and pizza without the other knowing it. And we both forgot the honey mustard dressing on the counter.

The city of Victoria greeted me the next morning with a rare snowfall; I stepped outside to a cobalt blue sky and a forest of trees carpeted by a two-foot layer of white. This was the stuff of Christmas cards. Not icky freezing rain, but the fluffy, picture-perfect kind that twinkled in the sun. The frigid temperatures did not deter me. After all, it was not sprinkling as Sam had predicted it would be. The unplowed roads thwarted our sightseeing plans, but Hett and I embarked on a hike through a three-hundred-acre wooded estate near her house. Thanks to her "quick little shortcut" we slogged back to her house through knee-high snow, arriving home an hour later.

After thawing out our limbs, we strolled to her health club where we soaked in the hot tub, slid down the water slide, and splashed in the pool. Unlike our teen episode in Paris, we were able to find the lockers where we had stashed our belongings. Then we strolled to the hairstyling salon for matching trims, where we had the stylists to ourselves since everyone else was snowed in.

On day two we hit the historical district of Victoria. To lure last-minute Christmas shoppers risking the elements, stores were offering irresistible deals. We leapt over piles of now-melting slush, soaking our shoes but too excited about our jewelry bargains to care about the tingling in our toes.

That evening, we visited with Mark's relatives for a white elephant exchange where we attempted to switch identities as well as gifts. Hett and I managed to fool a few of Mark's aunts and I succeeded in unloading the cleaver knife I had chosen first, thus avoiding a future scene at the airport.

For the trip home I was becoming suspicious. The holiday had gone a little too smoothly so far. I stepped on the right bus to the terminal; the driver smiled and waived the fee. There was room for me and my bag. Everything fit into my carry-on and I had remembered to remove all forbidden liquids, finally accepting the fact that a half-empty six-ounce tube would not be seen as three ounces.

Since Christmas was two short days away I fully expected to see a line snaking toward the ticket counters. An airport volunteer asked me where I was heading and asked me to step out of line. He pointed me towards the international terminal. I flashed my ID and moved forward to see what awaited me beyond the set of double doors.

The immigration officer studied my driver's license with the bad perm from ten years before and waved me through. Surely I would find throngs of people, like an Asian tour group teleported into the line with mounds of luggage. But the security area was deserted. I passed through and the agent wished me a nice trip.

"Where is everyone?" I asked her.

"You should have seen it earlier," she said.

I had heard that one before, only luck was on my side this time. Could it hold up? I walked toward my gate, glancing over my shoulder. No one was behind me. It was almost eerie.

Due to severe weather, the majority of flights into the Vancouver and Seattle area had been delayed or cancelled. I checked the Departures screen for outbound flights for San Francisco. The top part of the monitor read "CANCELLED, CANCELLED... The bottom part read CANCELLED, CANCELLED...

Lit up in the center of the list was my flight, UNITED FLIGHT 5114...ON TIME.

I could scarcely believe my good fortune—I had avoided major snowstorms in both directions. Vancouver and Seattle each shut down their airport—the day after I left.

Four months later our family flew to South Carolina to treat Sam's parents to a four-night stay at a beachfront condo in Charleston. I wanted my kids to enjoy their Nana and Granddad while they were still in reasonable health. I risked Easter weekend travel and a layover in Houston. Once again I avoided carnage in both directions: thunder storms, hailstorms, tornadoes, flight cancellations, and airport closures. On the flight leaving Houston we witnessed a bird's-eye view of a dazzling lightening show over the Gulf, from the safety of a few hundred miles away.

A cold drizzle on the first day evolved into perfect temperatures in the mid-to-high seventies. I arranged for my older sister, Peggy, to join us and she gladly escaped the demands of work and a long Canadian winter. We giggled over our chase with a supersized "Palmetto Bug" and marveled at two-hundred year old Spanish Oak trees and historic mansions. No, we didn't fit in everything I had hoped to do, but Nana remained healthy enough to stay the whole time and that is what I prayed for. She reminded me of the joy of living in the moment and Granddad exemplified to me love and devotion in marriage.

Should these trips have been included in the book if nothing went amiss? Yes, because it shows how rich life can be when we choose to "get on the plane" and take time to invest in the people around us. Knowing what could go wrong makes it that much more special when... all ends well!

Are We Having Fun Yet?—The Joys of Traveling with Kids

With the hassles of flying these days, it is almost easier to drive. That is, until someone pipes up from the back seat, "I have to pee"—fifty miles from the nearest freeway exit. Isn't it odd how we used to travel across the country without a second thought, but now with kids a trip across town evolves into a major expedition? Lewis and Clark probably carried less baggage on their 4000-mile historic trek to the Pacific Ocean. We are lucky if we can even find our Rand McNally atlas. Typically, we discover a crucial corner shredded off or covered in ketchup just as we approach a key junction.

When I was young, my family used to cross the country in an over-stuffed station wagon with five kids, a dog, and an old army tent for a week of camping at Myrtle Beach, South Carolina. (Having reenacted that trip with my twin and our five kids, in the luxury of a rented Ford Expedition, I can now appreciate that endeavor.) When I was a kid the only circulation came from the rush of warm air through the hand-cranked windows and the panting of our overheated dog.

Along the way we pulled out a trusted Nancy Drew or Hardy Boys book, or engaged in various contests to count objects we passed on the road. Imagine our cousins' surprise when they once spotted their own trailer passing them on the shoulder, after detaching itself from the car.

AFTER MONTHS OF PLANNING, *THE* DRISCOLL'S TRIP TO THE LAKE WENT OFF WITHOUT A HITCH

In the days before air bags, siblings argued for front-row seats to get first dibs on exciting roadside attractions. Now our kids fight over DS cartridges and DVDs, and all are craning their necks for a view of the TV—hopefully all but the driver. Cars are becoming more like airplanes on wheels minus the baggage restrictions, the weight limit, and the Call buttons. I'm not sure which passengers demand more attention but at least when traveling by air the seats are pre-assigned. Sam's parents avoided the front seat debate by taping a timer on top of the dashboard and setting a time limit for each of their five kids.

When getting in the spirit of a long road trip, it is helpful to rent such classics as Chevy Chase's *National Lampoon's Vacation*, about a family's riotous road trip from Chicago to L.A. to visit "Wally World" and to view the world's largest ball of string. My favorite scene is when Clark's aunt, squished in the back seat between two surly teens, expires along the way and he straps her to the roof of the car. It has crossed my mind to send one of our boys up top while they are fighting, but our storage rack lacks a sturdy set of seat belts.

It certainly could be easier to fly. That is, until we arrive at the airport. Traveling by air today involves as many delays as a Los Angeles freeway on a Friday night. With the required advance boarding time, we could be halfway across the country by the time we step on the plane. After we have endured the strip search, removed our shoes, tossed the contraband sunscreen and water bottles that I stuffed in Kyle's half-empty carry-on and all bags have cleared the X-ray machine, the kids are ready to go home. Naturally bladders are triggered as soon as the flight attendant closes the doors for takeoff or the "Fasten Your Seatbelt" sign lights up. One can only hope that the stewards will clear the aisle of the food cart in time to reach the restroom.

One tactical vacation error is scheduling too much fun. In today's era of jam-packed, structured activities, it is not unusual for a family to sandwich into a five-day trip a tour of Disneyland, LEGOLAND, SeaWorld, and the San Diego Zoo. My kids have still not made it to Disneyland; the fact that they don't realize what they're missing makes me think I'm not doing too badly as a mom. Or are they really missing something?

Never mind that it might take an hour to enter the park or require a second mortgage to pay the parking and admission fares. We will then have to deal with sensory overload as we corral past waves of fellow vacationers, all of whom share identical moods and travel itineraries. No matter when we choose to enter the park, everyone else will have the same idea at the same time.

When we finally arrive to the front of the line after melting in the sun for forty minutes, the ride will spit out passengers two minutes later. Then we will consult our maps and rejoin the weary masses for more thrills. For refreshment, we might sneak out the snacks buried in our bags, if they were not confiscated at the gate. Or we will join another line to pay $6 for a Mickey Mouse cup. (The cup may come in handy later after surveying the line to the bathroom.) As the sun drops in the sky we will stumble out the park with sunburned shoulders and souvenir cups. If we time the departure just right, the boys will be tired enough to be willing to leave but too tired to tease each other. We will sigh with relief that the kids did not get lost in the maze of the park, and helped us find our van amid the sea of SUVs, saving us the humiliation of calling security or waiting for everyone else to drive away.

I vote for a return to nature for our next trip. One of our most memorable vacations was the week we spent searching for snow during an August heat wave. We tumbled down sleds on Mount Lassen, California, swam in the shadow of snowy Mount Shasta, and tossed snowballs in Crater Lake National Park. From there we drove to Eastern Oregon where we hiked along fields of obsidian and lava tubes in the high desert region, saw glaciers atop Mount Bachelor, and splashed in alpine lakes at sunset.

The boys' vacation highlights include catching fish from a riverbank in Kauai with bamboo fishing pools purchased from the general store, and combing tide pools for crabs and starfish. Sam's favorite activity is to soar along the coast in his paraglider, peering down at us on the beach below.

Whether we prefer outings by land or by sea, in the air or on a riverbank, life is full of surprises. Recently I talked my friend Val into ditching chores to take her boys fishing with Nico and me at Loch Lomond, a jewel of a lake an hour from home. After the ranger helped us untangle the rods and attach the right hooks and lures, we headed off to the dock. Val's ten-year-old son eventually grew restless over not catching anything and wandered up the bank. "If fishing were easy it would be called catching," I reminded him. Determined, Jeremy sought a new spot to cast his line. He thrust his rod way back and released. The hook soared high into the sky and became embedded in a tree branch. Val and I took turns poking it free with a stick, joking "This could make it onto *America's Funniest Home Videos*." Just as she reached for her camera, I stumbled over a log and slid down the embankment—right into the water. Who says fishing can't be fun?

Wherever we choose to play, let's put the technology toys aside. Then again, have that video camera ready: who knows what will earn the $10,000 prize? Either way, memories are priceless.

6 ⁓ Decide What Matters Most

Where Did I Leave That?—Losing Your Things Without Losing Your Mind

Nothing raises blood pressure faster than a lost wallet or a set of car keys. These are the essentials we cannot go far without. My dependable husband has a system for everything so he never experiences the thrill of discovering missing items, except for the odd stray Easter egg. Before every plane trip Sam will ask, "Do you have the most important things: ID and a credit card? Everything else you can buy when you get there."

My wallet used to get around even more than I did. Once it was pilfered from my purse as I boarded a plane in Phoenix, and resurfaced behind a ticket booth in San Francisco. I wondered if it at least flew first class. Now I only carry as much as I am willing to lose or have stolen at one time.

On one occasion my wallet became the star of a Christmas Day miracle near my parents' hometown of Strathroy, Ontario. On Christmas Eve I accompanied them on a drive to visit my sister Marijke, two hours away. While passing through the town of Parkhill, I impulsively stopped at a quaint craft store to buy last-minute gifts. Having inherited my mom's ability to befriend a stranger in five minutes, the gregarious shop owner and I bantered amicably, until my parents lured me away with an offer of a free lunch. Between the quiche and apple pie, I marveled at the foot of snow that had accumulated outside the café. In one hour, the crunchy brown grass was covered by a carpet of white that grew plusher by the minute.

We stepped out into the winter wonderland, sparkling in the noonday sun. My California kids whizzed down the hill while we wiped off the thick white layer now draping our vehicle. Piling back into the car, we quickly abandoned our original mission to visit Marijke when the tires began swerving in a swirl of drifts. Safety trumped sociability. We turned our wipers to the highest setting, as they swished furiously back and forth to clear an open patch of window.

The next morning I reached into my purse for my wallet to ensure that I had the proper IDs for the flight home in twenty-four hours. I searched every pocket of my purse. Next, I rummaged through my ski jacket pockets and pulled up an old boarding pass and a few cookie crumbs. Family members descended upon the store where the wallet was last used and steps were retraced to my former parking spot. After we combed the streets for an hour and a half with a rake, it was finally spotted at the edge of town, where it had been shoved into a bank by the county snow plow.

For Christmas I traded the purse and wallet for a small leather tote with a built-in billfold, one that did not have fourteen pockets (these are probably designed by men to torment women).

My twin teases me about my mishaps, but let me report here that she has her own share of adventures that rival comedy routines. Once, while purchasing items at a checkout stand, Hett set her keys on a table-height box beside her. As the teller deposited her cash, Hett rummaged through her purse and searched the floor to see what had become of them. In walked a delivery man with a dolly, jingling a set of keys. "I found these while I was loading my truck." Who knows what adventures her keys could have had driving around the city while Hett crawled under clothing racks sucking up dust bunnies.

One mom I met in San Simeon, California was less fortunate when her keys disappeared on the beach. Determined not to let this quandary ruin her first major road trip with her ten-year-old son, she proceeded to tell me what a terrific time they were having. I loved how she chose not to dwell on the fact that a tow truck had to haul her car to the Mazda dealership an hour away while a new key was made, and that she kept a smile on her face despite her little setback.

(This lesson served me well when I was trying to impress my Canadian nephews in Sam's convertible and accidentally locked the keys inside.)

At times the vehicle becomes the culprit. Cars have a way of gobbling up crucial items in some Bermuda Triangle, usually when traveling solo with kids for maximum stress effect. Such was the case when I boarded a boat to attend a weeklong family camp on Catalina Island, not realizing till I was on the ferry that my wallet had slipped out of my purse under the driver's seat. How would I pay for emergency staples like chocolates, books and tampons? The camp director kindly took an I-O-U and reminded me of priorities. "Did anybody die? Is the world ending today? Do you know where you are spending eternity?"

The bigger worry for my kids might have been losing their Internet connection, but this technology-free week demonstrated to all of us what really mattered in life. We soaked in the heavenly surroundings without the earthly distractions and reunited with the wallet upon our return.

The less we have, the less we have to lose—and the more careful we are not to lose it in the first place. Such was the case with Nico's former can't-sleep-without-it blankie, which I used to search for often amidst returned shopping carts. (Now he is old enough to remind me where I left the cart and to steer me away from potential distractions.)

There are few things of value that cannot be replaced, except for our families. As far as missing wallets, now I ask myself, "What's the worst thing that could happen—stolen identity?" I'm not sure who would dare to be me—except for my twin.

What Else Could Go Wrong?—Confessions of a Drama Queen

"Your life is so interesting," my friends used to tell me. A little drama not only adds interest but suspense when you never know what curveball to expect next. This is true both at work and at home. Poor sleep, aging cars, uncertain jobs, and tight finances can all conspire to push us over the edge.

Take, for example, the following unembellished account of a former week in the Linton household. While this wacky season seems a lifetime ago from the mostly sunny days we now enjoy, the memories remain as fresh as yesterday. I can tell it's shaping up to be an "interesting" week when...

Monday:
1. The brake sensor is screeching that it's time for new brake pads, but I can't move my car off the driveway because the ignition is stuck.
2. The tow truck driver informs me that, because the ignition is jammed and the wheels are locked, I must wait two hours for a locksmith.
3. My husband calls from the side of the road to say his vehicle has died and he is waiting for a tow truck to bring it home.
4. I enter the garage to fold a mountain of laundry and a rat leaps out of the dog food bag. I squeal, slam the door, and ration my remaining clean clothes, for fear of facing more furry friends.
5. The furnace repairman comes to clean the air ducts and drops debris into the halogen lamp, creating the foundation for a campfire

in the living room. My six-year-old son Kyle casually mentions that the lamp has caught fire as smoke starts curling towards the ceiling.

6. After spending $200 to diagnose the ailing camper van, we decide it's not worth fixing anymore, and a Sasquatch-size man from a domestic violence nonprofit removes it from our driveway. (The kids spent only one night in it and have no memory of the family bonding camping experience.)

7. I ask Sam if he cares to have people over for his birthday that weekend, or if he prefers a quiet weekend, and he replies, "That's a no-brainer." Then I quickly un-invite all the people I just invited for his surprise 40th birthday party.

That was *Monday*.

Tuesday:
The power goes off for the entire day for no apparent reason.

Wednesday:
1. Sam is out of town so I am rushing to bring our first grader and his two-year-old brother to school before the second bell. Then it dawned on me that it is "Muffins for Moms" morning at school, a chance to meet other moms. Of the 200 people attending, I am the last to arrive, as the final muffin crumbs are being carried out the door. I am the only mom in sight who has not eaten.

2. I return home to fix the lunch I did not have time to prepare and drop it off at the school office. I try to pay the cafeteria for the $10 worth of hot lunches my son preferred over homemade ones, but the money has slipped from the pocket of my polyester dress pants.

3. It is finally my turn at the discount gas pump when I remember that my Costco card is in my dresser drawer and the needle on the gas meter reads "Empty."

Thursday:

1. Happily returning from a hunting and gathering mission for dinner, I bring in the take-out and forget the purse in the car. In the morning while searching for the purse, I discover that I left our dog Pixie in the car all night. To relieve herself, she peed all over the carpet, which we couldn't air out for two days due to torrential rains.

Friday:

1. I bravely enter my garage to retrieve the dog food. (Pixie had been forced to diet for several days due to my recurring fear of entering the garage.) Easing the door open, I discover a rodent on steroids suspended from the trap over the washing machine.

2. My water heater dies for good. It had been temporarily repaired so I could avoid taking all my showers at the YMCA. Half the strawberry shampoo bottle in my trunk spills next to an abandoned sippy cup, which at least helps clear the odor of the sour milk oozing from the cracked lid.

3. The new water heater arrives, along with an $800 bill. The washing machine floods the garage, leaving a soaking pile of previously clean, dry, and waiting-to-be-folded laundry.

The following Monday…

Things can only get better from here. Others have it much worse. I tell my mom, "At least Sam is employed."

1. Sam informs me that the wireless communications company he started two years before just lost their last source of funding as their venture capitalist had declared bankruptcy. Sam must lay off all twenty employees, himself included.

2. Returning from work, his car engine dies and the exhaust springs a leak.

Here we go again!

Even the not-so-funny-when-it-happened events in life can be savored when we remember those blessings we take for granted, like family and friends, a place to call home, good food to eat, and clean water to drink. Our perspective is sometimes so clouded from worry over past failings or future calamities, we fail to see the silver linings. For those who are just "hanging in there," remember that God never wants to leave us hanging. Compared to the life and death stresses that many face daily, we can still find lots to delight in.

What Channel Are You On?—The Perils of Communication

When Kyle started grade school I jumped at the chance to help out the secretary, Laura, in the office one morning. I much prefer helping others to being the one who needs help.

Her assistant was absent that day so she needed someone to fill in for half an hour. One concern caused me to hesitate but I decided that the outdoor temperature was cool enough that I did not need to worry.

"My dog is in the car, but I guess she'll be okay," I mentioned casually as I sat down to work. Half an hour later, Laura strolled back into the office with photocopies in hand, shooting me a quizzical look.

"Are you sure she's all right?" she queried, sitting down at her desk.

Seeing the concern etched in her brow I figured she was a real animal lover, not realizing that Laura thought it was my *daughter* I'd left in the car.

I rambled on, "Oh, she'll be fine. She likes staying in the car. I cracked the windows open so she can get some air."

Seeing that this fellow dog fan was looking increasingly perplexed, I reassured her, "I did leave some water for her. It's not that hot in there."

Looking rather skeptical, Laura inquired, "Are you sure she hasn't been in the car too long?"

"No, she's just happy to get out of the house," I replied. "She doesn't know any better—she never notices if it's a few minutes or a few hours. I do let her out to go to the bathroom," I chattered on.

Finally, Laura turned to me in relief, realizing, "Oh, you left your *dog* in the car!"

Thankfully, I avoided getting a call from children's protective services or the humane society. (Had they arrived they would have discovered that I had no car seat for the dog. At the rate the canine craze is going, I'm sure that will come next.)

Life is rife with overlooked cues and misunderstandings. At times I wonder, *Did I miss something? How did this dialog take such a wrong turn?*

At times we wonder if everyone else is on a different channel. Like the time Hett once watched half an airplane movie on the first-class audio channel that started five minutes after economy class, and wondered why all the characters displayed such delayed reactions to impending doom.

I used to accuse Sam of not hearing correctly even before the distractions of raising children. One incident sent him to the doghouse for a year. (I am quicker to forgive now.)

We were driving to Lake Del Valle in Livermore, California, where Sam planned to give his friend Pat a windsurfing lesson. Pat occupied the front passenger tinted-window seat while I sat in back, where the sun beat upon my head. We stopped to buy gas at the last station before the freeway entrance, and I casually informed Sam, "I'm getting a drink. I'll be right back."

I sauntered to the soft drink machine in search of a caffeine-free beverage. I pressed the button. The can dropped to the bottom with a satisfying thud. Chilled can in hand, I turned toward the car, only to see it rolling away from the gas pump.

Sam is so considerate moving out of the way for someone else to fill up, I mused. "Oh sh—!" He's leaving!"

I watched, open-jawed, as our car merged into traffic. Snapping out of my slow-motion reverie, I leapt into action. Like a cat after prey, I sprinted after him. Sam can't dump me that easily.

By then he was dangerously close to the freeway on-ramp, unaware of the empty back seat. I veered down the middle of the road, hoping to attract his attention on the driver's side. Just then he glanced in the rearview mirror to see a mad woman dashing down the median.

"That doesn't look very safe," he mentioned to Pat. Then the realization sank in. "OH MY GOSH! That's Yvonne!"

This "sin" surely rates as worse than leaving the dog in the car. I finally forgave Sam after he e-mailed me a news story about an Italian spouse who inadvertently abandoned his wife at a rest stop in Europe. He drove on with the children, never noticing her absence. Several hours and three countries later, a policeman pulled him over to inform him of his error.

I wonder if they are still married.

What is it with husbands and wives? We progress from hanging spellbound on every word in the early days of marriage to year seven, not even noticing that our beloved is missing from the car.

This brings to mind another useful tool for staying on the same wavelength—instant messaging. In an attempt to improve communication, my dear husband installed Yahoo's instant messaging service on my computer. Now I have the convenience of having icons popping up with pinging noises when I am deep in a computer trance.

"Hope I'm not interrupting you," read one.

I did not recognize the user name.

"Don't mean to bother you," it beeped on. "I live in the Bay Area, too. Do you want to connect?"

Who is this creep and why is he writing to me?

Then I remember: I had filled out a Yahoo Group Profile for a Mountain Biking Club the previous year in an attempt to find a biking partner. This backfired when a dyke on a (motor) bike wrote back, "Interested in a little hot passion?"

Irked, I fired off an e-mail to my latest suitor, "I don't know who you are, and I don't have time to e-mail you," to which he replied, "Technically I'm not e-mailing you. And a simple 'no' would have sufficed."

(I had not received so much online communication since I impersonated my single twin on a free trial of eHarmony, a Christian dating service. Within twenty-four hours I had a flurry of men from New Mexico to Hawaii requesting letters and photos.)

The next day I received another instant message.

"Are you single?" it read.

It was from Sam.

I still vote for old-fashioned face-to-face communication to ensure that everyone is on the same channel and we can inform our partners of our latest activities and whereabouts. But maybe we should leave cell phones turned on in case we find ourselves stranded and need to send a text message with GPS coordinates. Or, if you see a frowning face standing at the side of the road, please alert the highway patrol.

I'm coming after you, Sam!

The Extracurricular Treadmill—Where Have All the Children Gone?

Apart from our spouses, little in life is more precious than our children. However, children aren't just raised anymore; they are programmed.

It begins before birth. Classical melodies penetrate the womb while Junior is trying to sleep. Babies come out humming Beethoven's Fifth Symphony. They are propped up with stimulating accessories of all shapes and sizes, strategically dangling in front of their car seats, cribs, and bouncy chairs.

As children approach the tender preschool age, the search for the right preschool begins. Schools are carefully examined for their academic rigor. Who has time for the "developmental" approach? The best-reputed schools have moms or dads staked out with tents and Coleman stoves hours before the 6AM opening. This is serious business. There is no time to play; there is too much material to cover. We dare not fall behind.

Children are expected to be almost literate by the time they reach kindergarten—if they are not burnt out by then. Teacher reputations and test scores are at stake.

"What were you thinking, sending your child to school with an August birthday?" (If only you had been in the mood sooner, you could have conceived at the right time?)

"Here is a stack of fifty flashcards to practice in the evenings," my friend was advised.

Now we must do remedial work at home, sandwiched between hours of extracurricular activities. It starts with "Mommy and Me" water classes. In the past we simply tossed our babies in the pool to see if Junior would sink or swim. Baby gymnastics classes are now added to the list of skills to acquire. Shortly thereafter, dance lessons begin. In between memorizing lines for theater, kids master kung fu and karate. If there is time left over, tennis and music lessons are thrown into the mix. By the time the child reaches high school, he is playing three instruments.

We don't just need a calendar to schedule our child's activities; we need a Blackberry with an alarm bell to remind us of where to show up next. Shuttling our kids to their activities by the start of the session is even more challenging than learning a new sport. And then we have to get them home.

When Kyle was in the under-twelve soccer league, I ran into an old friend near the practice field. After reviewing the highlights and lowlights of the last two years, my mind turned to more practical concerns like dinner plans. I headed off to the store, and soon my cell phone rang.

"Weren't you just at the field?" Coach Mike asked. "Are you coming back for Kyle?"

Kyle never noticed I had gone.

Who is more confused: the children or us parents?

Kids are cajoled to the car and crammed into cleats, tights, and bathing suits. For moms, the biggest sports accomplishment is finding all the matching pieces of the uniform. Despite my stint on the MIT women's ice hockey team, I have not introduced my kids to the sport because we have no room at home for all the gear.

One mom I know had her van stolen with all the equipment inside. The thought of replacing all the gear upset her even more than losing the van and the extra storage space it provided.

Cars have become an extension of our houses. If they are not used for storing things, they are used for homework rooms and dining areas. Meals are consumed in the car between fast food restaurants and practices, and school assignments are scribbled between potholes and U-turns. Between bites, we attempt to discover how the day went, but everyone is too tired or hurried to reply.

"Why are we doing all this?" we might ask if only we had time to stop and think.

If kids are not signed up for an activity, they will become "hooked on television and computer screens." We worry about them packing on the pounds, becoming anti-social, or not having anything to fill in on their college application forms.

One Silicon Valley teen wrote to *Dear Abby* bemoaning her lack of free time: "I practice every day for swim team. I take German lessons because my mom thinks I need a foreign language for the pre-SAT tests. My passion is sailing club and I don't want to give that up. I enjoy my violin lessons three days a week and I play in an orchestra. I am maintaining my A average but I'm starting to feel stressed because I have no time for myself." Small wonder!

To stay fit ourselves while hurrying our kids to every practice, we can join a host of classes as well: aerobics, kickboxing, Pilates. Yet many of us exercise so sporadically that our gym memberships become charitable donations each month. When I asked one mom what she did for exercise, I was met with a blank stare.

For me the highlight of Nico's soccer season is the end-of-the-year party when parents face off in a scrimmage against the children. What a blast! It makes me wonder why I even keep my gym membership when I can play for free with my children. No more watching the action from the sidelines. Parents with rusty muscles delight in catapulting the ball down the field. Positions are tossed to the wind and players are not restricted to any amount. Kids mercilessly dribble the ball around panting parents who stand like pegs in a pinball machine. Somehow the ball always finds its way into the net—perhaps the coaches do *too* good a job.

With all the programs our children participate in, let's remember what they need most. When pressures loom, throw convention aside. Play with your kids and discover the kid in you. (Nico recommends twenty minutes a day.)

Remember to warm up first and don't forget the Ben-Gay.

Pampered Pets—Caring for Our Furry Friends

We pamper our animals sometimes even more than we do our children. Americans spend over $40.8 billion on our pets, more than twice what Canada spends on its entire defense budget, and more than the gross domestic product of 60 percent of the world's nations. At least we do not have to put our pets through college.

Pet health plans are becoming a routine employee benefit. If our employees were valued as much as our animals, the economy might be in better shape. What wouldn't we do for our furry family members?

A friend recounted the final days of her rat, Espresso, sister to Cappuccino. (If there's anything we love more than our pets, it's our coffee.) She was becoming blind and riddled with tumors and arthritis.

"Any one of these problems I could treat, but not all three," the vet announced somberly. "I think it is best we put her down."

Imagine surgery to remove a tumor on a rodent. The rat joined the cat whose final resting place lay in the back yard. This brings up the delicate issue of what to do with our pets when they reach their demise.

A California woman sought regulation for the pet crematorium industry. It appears that the ashes of her seven-pound purebred poodle, Fifi, belonged instead to a twenty-five pound mutt.

FIFI GETS EVEN

"Mixing up the remains has only happened about half a dozen times in the last ten years," the president of Bubbling Well Pet Memorial Park assured her.

What if that pet were your relative? The bereaved owner of the lost pooch lamented, "She was not just a dog to me, she was my girl."

Surely something must be done to prevent further travesties. I first stumbled upon Bubbling

Well while cycling through the bucolic hills of the Napa wine country during my free weekend at the spa. My only concern at the time was where to find a bathroom. Little did I know I had stumbled upon the largest pet cemetery in America. I only hope that someday my final resting place offers so fine a view.

Casting furtive glances toward the office, I infiltrated the chapel where comforting tones of soothing melodies filled the air. Boxes of Kleenex were strategically planted around the room. Along one wall stood a row of silk-lined coffins and an array of granite markers. An ornate collection of urns and engraved wooden boxes for ashes sat in a display next to it. I marveled that few people could afford such a lavish farewell for their loved ones, much less their pets. Such a send-off probably costs more than many foreign laborers earn in a year.

I found the restroom and snuck back out the door with suspicious pets sniffing after me. I hopped back on my bike, pondering the future of my own aging dog.

Pixie, otherwise known as Pigsy, had faced death before. Over Christmas vacation, we had boarded her with our trusted vet. We'd sent her off with a slight hobble. As with many health afflictions, we hoped the problem would disappear by itself. Upon our return, they notified us of an increased limp. This prompted an X-ray that revealed a shaded area. The vet filling in for the holidays suspected bone cancer. With hardly a pause for us to absorb the dire prognosis, he told us what to expect in her last days and handed us a $100 bill and a $50 pain prescription. In her last days, she deserved the best. We purchased the special aging-dog kibbles and, in our grief, accidentally grabbed the cat food instead. A dog that devoured anything in sight, including soap, sponges, and sanitary napkins, Pixie never knew the difference.

We broke the news of Pixie's impending demise to the kids who, thankfully, did not flee to their rooms in a torrent of tears. For her final days they resolved to walk her more often than once a year. This lasted about a week. Soon it became clear that our pudgy but perky Pixie was still very much alive, judging from the way she pounced with Olympic agility whenever food appeared. Our regular vet returned and diagnosed a mere infection, which a round of antibiotics quickly cleared up. We all breathed sighs of relief.

Happily, she went on to live for several more years, eventually passing away peacefully in the night, sparing us the trauma of putting her to sleep.

One pet I have learned to "just say no" to are mice and rats, until one summer when I made the mistake of watching a pair of odiferous rodents for a teacher friend. Her husband said she would divorce her if she brought home the class pet again, so I stepped in to save the marriage.

The mice were supposed to have been frogs; one of her six-year-old students brought the wrong animals to class. (Apparently they had not yet studied that part of the animal kingdom.) I stocked the rodents' food and water receptacles generously, and upgraded their accommodations to a large cage with an elaborate network of tunnels. For the first few days, they frolicked about as if on an all-expense paid trip to Club Med. When one mouse's musky smell became unbearable, I banished them both to the garage—until the heat wave hit. I relocated them to the breezy side yard, careful to erect a shady canopy overhead. Then the sun moved.

Only the fittest survived. The smelliest one probably met a swifter end than the hamster who disappeared in Sam's childhood home. His parents did not discover its remains until winter, when the furnace started up. How can we ensure the health and safety of our loved ones? One local vet suggested an exercise program. Shedding our own pounds is enough of a challenge. Could this be the start of a new trend: pet aerobics? Spas could offer fitness services beyond the current offerings of "pawdicures" and aromatherapy baths, and deck the dogs in terry cloth robes or silk pajamas (now available online). Or if the workout is too strenuous for them, there are pet bodybuilding formulas, obesity pills, and plenty of dog walkers—some of whom earn six-figure salaries.

Occasionally, unsuspecting friends or family members agree to watch pets while owners go on vacation. Even a nursing degree hardly prepares them for such a potential list of maladies. They end up having to inject cats with insulin, coax down heartworm pills for dogs, dispense seizure meds, and prepare gourmet meals. My twin once was instructed to feed a mouse to her son's snake, Simon. He snubbed the frozen fare she first offered him, so she heated the mouse up in the microwave. Soon after, Simon escaped from his cage, whose top Hett had forgotten to replace. No doubt, he was seeking a tastier meal elsewhere.

Since the next best thing for health is a good night's sleep, websites also offer our furry friends orthopedic and heated mattresses and feathered French day beds for optimal comfort. If these swank bedding options fail to revive our pup, high-end pet stores like The Barkery in Scottsdale offer $500 cologne for Fido to freshen up, or doggy make-up is available from Lush Puppy in Las Vegas to help with those unflattering bags under the eyes.

Ever since our new dog, Stacy, has taken to sneaking under our comforter during the night, it is my bags that need covering. I rarely use cosmetics myself—if I do Sam wonders if I am dressing up for Halloween or joining the witness protection program. When I started to spend more on my dog's hair than my own, I decided it was time to upgrade from Supercuts and Suave shampoo, stopping short of perfumes and silk bows.

Animal psychologists and chiropractors stand by ready to help, should our pets get overtaxed from all this coddling. For all the joy they give us over the years, they deserve it, don't they?

Dads are no longer the top dogs. My real estate agent once called to review a list of potential tenants for our rental property: A mom, two kids, a dog... and a husband, relegated to an afterthought. Canine and feline companions have become the third child; in San Francisco, dogs outnumber kids two to one. The next thing you know, they'll be permitted in the carpool lane.

Our animals may peck at our plates, scarf our scraps, sleep on our satin sheets, and pilfer our pillows, but we love them. As pets become a treasured part of our families, their welfare takes on increasing importance. Thousands of dollars might be offered to locate a lost pet or nurse it back to health, yet when our kids start fighting in the car we are ready to drop them off at the side of the road.

How can we say no to our pets when they look at us with those adoring eyes? Should we limit the amount of prescriptions and pampering—or do whatever it takes to keep them happy? They say pets lower our cholesterol and our blood pressure. If they save our health *and* our sanity, surely we can't put a price on that.

Want Fries with That?—The Fight for Fitness

If losing weight were an Olympic sport, I'd fare worse than the Jamaican bobsled team. Even a child on Christmas morning shows more self-restraint. I am like the woman in the picture that reads "I was on a diet for two weeks and all I lost was two weeks."

When my sons began wondering if they were getting a new brother or sister, I decided to take action. Didn't I owe it to my family to look and feel my best? Was it time to check out the weight loss centers? I conceal my middle-aged spread quite well under strategically layered outfits, but I was self-conscious about entering a room full of "foodies" at the nearest weight loss center.

Am I chubby enough?

In my quest to beat the statistic of adding one pound a year after marriage, I shied away from the group therapy approach and weigh-ins of Weightwatchers and headed to the nearest Jenny Craig outlet. Here they pile you up with enough frozen food varieties to make you desperate for a home-cooked meal. The consultant's bosom practically exploded out of her low-cut sweater, as she leaned over to describe the prepared meal options in mouth-watering terms.

MY NEW YEAR'S RESOLUTION IS TO BE THE IDEAL WEIGHT FOR MY HEIGHT... WHAT DO YOU HAVE WITH SIX-INCH HEELS?

offthemark.com ATLANTIC FEATURE © 2000 MARK PARISI

I tactfully asked, "Are you still seeing results from the Jenny Craig system?"

"After my baby was born," she replied evasively.

I resisted the urge to ask how old the baby was now, since she obviously had packed on a few extra calories since then. This was hardly an inspiring testimonial for weight loss maintenance. I resorted to other means.

Why do we find it so difficult to stay motivated in our exercise routines, and justify it by claiming that the pounds will climb right back on?

To answer this question, I delved into the complex subject of motivation, looking to various athletes for inspiration. I attended a Leukemia Team and Training Information session and listened to inspirational tales of overweight and ill people conquering triathlons, marathons, and century rides. What keeps the average person going? What possesses a swimmer to plunge in the pool at five in the morning? What inspires a woman to train for a marathon on a treadmill in Alaska? How does a person handle the inevitable setbacks that make it so much more inviting to throw in the towel?

I questioned Olympic athletes. Few people display the stick-to-it spirit of the former University of Texas athlete I talked to named Shaun Jordan. I had read his story in a *Sports Illustrated for Kids* book; he was called "Scrawn" by his varsity swim coach and benched the entire first year until he bulked up. Finally he had a chance to compete in a big college meet at Berkeley. He perched in the starting blocks, peeled off his final layer of protection against pelting rain, and dove into the choppy water. As he broke the surface, his bathing suit slid in the opposing direction, coming to a stop between his knees and his ankles.

In dogged determination "the man in white" paddled on, to the cheers of the announcer, classmates, and the competing team. Shaun not only helped his team rally from last to second place in the meet, he went on to win gold at the 1988 Summer Olympics in Seoul and the 1992 Olympics in Barcelona.

We don't all have Olympic drive, but we can hop in the pool. Secretly, I eye the YMCA pool deck hoping the lanes are too overcrowded or some kid has had a bathroom emergency forcing everyone to evacuate. But once I set a goal, I can usually crawl out of my cozy warm clothes and paddle at a faster pace than the senior water aerobics class.

Inspired by a thirty-six-year-old Leukemia Team in Training athlete I met named Louie Bonpua, I began preparing for my first triathlon in 2001. At the height of his leukemia treatment—when he could barely stagger from his bathroom to the living room couch—Louie decided he would one day enter the San Francisco Alcatraz Triathlon. Preferring to be a participant than an honoree, Louie went on to complete six triathlons in one year and an Ironman competition (112-mile bike ride, 2.4-mile swim, and 26-mile run) within the last months of his life. His final victory was carrying the Olympic Torch on its way to Salt Lake City, after which he lapsed into a coma and never awakened.

If Louie could accomplish superhuman feats, then surely I could complete a little triathlon. Feeling sporty in my high-top Speedo, I sprinted into the lake, thrusting my thighs high and thinking of Louie. I was soon surrounded by swarms of thrashing arms. A few brave souls resorted to the backstroke in an effort to stay afloat; it was all I could do to avoid being whacked in the head.

After pulling my biking shorts on over my bathing suit, I grabbed my bike from a sea of wheels and eagerly approached the twenty-five mile biking portion. Initially I kept a safe but chatting distance with the cyclist peddling next to me, but must have slowed her down too much, for she sighed at her stop watch and lunged ahead.

During the running portion I staggered in the noonday heat as temperatures soared into the high nineties. My ego plummeted faster than a present down the chimney as I watched two Santa-haired ladies breeze by. I trudged on for six miles. *They've obviously been doing these events much longer*, I comforted myself.

Hopefully this was benefitting my muscles, if not my morale. I wondered about all the people who motivate themselves through one humbling performance after the next.

After recovering my pride, I contacted Stanford swimming coach and Olympic coach, Richard Quick, to learn more about the psyche of athletes. He regaled me with stories of swimmers and what set winners apart.

"Winners accept plateaus and down times as temporary setbacks and not as something that will keep happening," he told me. "They make a critical decision at the critical moment and have the ability to move on."

Every attitude involves a decision. Eventually we must decide what success means for us, and which road to take to arrive there. (Quick's former protégé, Angie Wester-Krieg, found success in fourth place after six Olympic trials. Success for her teammate, Dara Torres, included medaling at the Sydney Olympics after a seven-year absence from swimming—and returning from her fifth Olympics with a silver medal at the age of forty-one.)

While I never manage to keep the pounds off permanently, I lost enough inches off my waist that summer to fill a Goodwill rack. Starting out, I could barely survive ten minutes in the pool nor could I push my bike up a pitch in the road. But eventually my arms and legs no longer felt like cannons and I worked up to biking over a hundred miles in one day. Now I regularly ride up steep hills, swim in a neighborhood pool club, and take long walks.

My new walking partner is Stacy, our six-pound Chihuahua and Italian Greyhound mix who runs twelve miles per hour. My son Kyle is my diet enforcement officer, charging a dollar for each infraction and periodically subjecting me to the Wii Fit Sports fitness challenge.

Trimming off a few inches or completing or riding a hundred miles may seem like an Olympic-size goal, but whatever our dreams, we all have a shot at success if we are not so anxious to reach the finish line that we skip the smaller steps to get there. While most of us have more trouble squeezing into our bathing suit than having it fall off, we all appreciate the spirit of people like Shaun and Louie who had every reason to quit but chose not to. One thing is sure—if we fear defeat, we will never even dare to get wet.

What's for Dinner?—The Dreaded Domestic Question

The one important decision that every household must face on a regular basis is, "What's for dinner?" Perhaps you possess a naturally gregarious disposition and a knack in the kitchen like Rachael Ray. You don your apron at a moment's notice and dish out healthy, mouth-watering delicacies for admiring diners. Your fridges and cupboards are always neatly stashed with key ingredients.

For some of us less organized chefs, our minds go blank as we dig through our recipe boxes and the splattered pages of our cookbooks for meals to match the few staples we have on hand. Despite all good intentions of choosing tantalizing recipes from *Sunset* magazines or *Good Housekeeping* subscriptions, we turn to the standbys we have come to rely on year after year. As long as our family does not leave the table hungry, isn't that matters most?

Q: DO I HAVE TO EAT THIS?
A: YES
Q: WHY?
A: IT'S GOOD FOR YOU
Q: CAN I HAVE SOMETHING ELSE?
A: NO
Q: THERE. DID I EAT ENOUGH?
A: NO
Q: HOW MANY MORE BITES?
A: SIX
Q: HOW ABOUT THREE?
A: SEVEN
Q: HOW ABOUT SIX?
A: OK

TO EXPEDITE DINNER, THE CLOUTMANS POSTED AN FAQ PAGE

Having children adds an extra challenge to cooking. The more time spent preparing the meal, the least likely a child will want to eat it.

"I don't like it," they lament before lifting fork to mouth.

If one eats only the noodles, another will prefer only sauce. Moms become short-order cooks to accommodate every family member.

No wonder dogs are becoming so chubby; they eat what no one else wants to polish off.

After visiting an organic farm that featured a traumatizing display of how chickens are drowned and zapped before coming to market, we had to pretend everything was pork. Thankfully Kyle, our bird-loving teen, will make an exception for corn dogs, as his vegetarian phase was limited to peanut butter and ketchup. Since the way to a man's heart is through his stomach, I keep feeding him whatever he craves most.

These days, stores and eateries have made it easy for the time-challenged and culinary-impaired. Crock-Pot ingredients and crêpes can be purchased in a bag. Salad ingredients come already assembled, wrapped in cute little pouches within a package. Fajitas come pre-made. Fruit is chopped up into cubes for us. My oven and Crock-Pot do not receive the same heavy use of my frying pan, as they require more advance planning. Everything can be made from a box—from French toast to scrambled eggs and even peanut butter and jelly sandwiches. Food companies take even the simplest fare and do the job for us. Convenience takes precedence over competence.

People are willing to endure long restaurant lines for the thrill of someone else serving a plate of food, even if they could have butchered and cooked a cow by the time the waitress arrives. Maybe the attraction is the element of surprise; one never quite knows what to expect when trying a new dining locale.

In the late '80s my brother-in-law Marv and his colleague were treating themselves to a rare break from their relief work in Haiti, eager to try out a new Western-style restaurant in town. Their stomachs growled in happy anticipation as the waiter arrived with Heineken bottles, quarter-pound burgers and French fries in hand. They slathered a pile of ketchup over their fries and burgers. Opening their mouths wide, they chomped into their burgers. Between chewing they continued their conversation about their latest community development project. All too soon they devoured half their hamburgers. It was then they noticed a flicker of movement in the ketchup bottle. Hesitantly they lifted their buns and peered inside. Maggots were swimming in a sea of ketchup. They downed a few swigs of beer in the hopes of drowning the maggot counterparts they had just consumed. Revolted, they asked the waiter for a refund.

"I give you only half since you ate half," he replied in broken English.

That made me feel better about the cockroach I once saw scurrying down the wall of a Bay Area restaurant, just as the waitress brought out the main course. I tried to distract my lunch companion so as not to spoil her appetite. Then again, isn't the protein the most important part?

Sam and I had all but quit dining out after one anniversary dinner, when artfully arranged items with fancy names concealed the congealed glob of gnocchi and rubbery rib-eye steak disappointment that followed. Our babysitter took pity afterwards and offered us her leftovers.

Home cooking took on a whole new attraction. But when time is lacking I turn to Trader Joe's: for barely more than the price of ingredients, you can purchase instant meals without the mountain of dishes that follows a cooking spree.

With all the instant meals available today, perhaps a frozen food culinary show would be popular. I can visualize it now: "First we peel back the cardboard corner. Cut off excess wrapping. We recommend you remove all packaging and place on a Corning dish to prevent Styrofoam or plastic from emitting chemicals during the heating process. Place frozen food in center of glass tray. Cooking time will vary based on the robustness of your microwave. If your dinner turns into a shriveled-up lump, you have nuked it too long."

Every microwave is designed differently so as not to remove the challenge of "cooking" entirely. (In the culinary world, this is actually referred to as *reheating*, not cooking.)

We can prevent fires in the kitchen, provided we do not fry the box or melt the plastic. Just in case, remember to replace the smoke alarm that you removed the last time the shrieking sounds sent you running from the stove.

When I was newly married and trying to impress Sam with my cooking skills honed in Paris, I set out to make falafels from scratch. I lovingly prepared the zesty little cannonball shapes and eased them into an oil-filled frying pan. It was a cast iron job of Civil War vintage, a gift from my mom. Momentarily distracted from the kitchen, I returned to find flames leaping from the burner. My heroic husband rushed to my aid, smothering the flames with a towel. Thankfully that did not catch fire as well, but the resulting smoke plumes forced him to relocate the spewing pan outdoors, burning his foot along the way. (This was a reflex from our days in Stanford student housing complex, where a crisis in the kitchen required a six-story building evacuation and a safety clearance from the campus fire department.)

With the bounty of budget ethnic take-outs in Northern California, it is almost a crime to cook. We are supporting the local economy to boot and using fundraiser entertainment coupons before they expire. So when inspiration or time is in short supply, I'm chucking the guilt over not creating a culinary masterpiece every night. I am bringing food to the table on time, so the kids no longer have to hold up picket signs saying "Want Food!" Dinner is just a freezer-full away.

7 ❖ Keep Things Simple

The Donut Debacle—Surviving Soccer Snack Duty

It all started with the donuts. What blunder could I possibly commit with a donut? I contemplated my past pitfalls as a soccer mom: registering late, sending my child to the field in unmatched socks, and accidentally leaving him at practice (after watching him play for an hour) topped the list. Infractions that followed close behind included uttering a sound during the recently enforced silent cheering days. This was an attempt to control outbursts from overzealous fans, which prompted the league to require parents to sign waivers promising to behave and to remain mute for one game. Another infraction is straying to the wrong side of the field. (Parents have now been separated from coaches.)

The final place to avoid a *faux pas* is on soccer snack duty. This is the part of the season where you provide treats to grabbing hands during half-time and immediately after the last whistle.

For my previous turn, I had carefully dispensed watermelon slices, which the kids consumed with reckless abandon. After tossing me their leftover rinds, they were so stuffed with water they could hardly sprint up the field for the rest of the game.

For my next snack duty I decided on the more traditional grapes and water. I shied away from the Gatorade that a mom recommended for kids to "replenish the fluids and electrolytes lost in play;" this was hardly the sort of collegiate-level competition to warrant concern over replacing bodily fluids.

The next important task was to choose an enticing array of end-of-game snacks. Having suffered the past embarrassment of forgetting to purchase the goods *before* the game, I was glad to remember my turn in advance. Resisting the urge to keep it simple, I caved to the pressure of finding the best victory or consolation prize. Previous moms had supplied colorful bags of treats tied with matching ribbons, chips, fruit roll-ups, and Rice Krispie squares. It wasn't just a snack anymore, it was a party.

I trotted off the local Safeway grocery store, looking for something that had not been "done" before. Combing the aisles, my eyes landed upon a sign in the bakery section advertising a dozen donuts on sale. (My kids say I will buy anything if it is on sale.) Risking potential disapproval from health-conscious moms for overdosing their children with white refined sugar products, I followed my impulse. My mouth watered at the spread of glistening donuts, pulled out of the oven moments before, invoking memories of my college donut-making job. So many options, how to decide? I scanned the delectable chocolate-coated and candy-sprinkled donuts, and imagined the look of bliss that would cross the children's faces as they were presented with such succulent treasures. I plucked out the maple donuts, jelly-filled donuts, custard-filled donuts, white-powdered, honey-glazed, sugar—I went for them all. No matter if kids would all seek the same kind; I chose two of every flavor. Figuring there were ten players on the team, and eight expected to play that day, I decided a dozen would be fine. Why purchase more than you need? Satisfied, I sealed up the box and took my stash to the cashier.

What could go wrong?

My halftime duties of dispensing water and grapes at halftime now completed, I resumed bantering with other moms on the appropriate sideline. All too soon the final whistle sounded, and I sprang into action to avoid the onslaught of hungry players clamoring for food. I sized up the crowd and carefully dispensed one donut to each child. A new group of hands appeared. "Hey, they're not even on our team!" one teammate protested. Noticing that their shirts were indeed a different color, I was thrown off my game thinking the snack was so popular that members of the next team were coming for a taste. Relieved that all the members on my son's team appeared to have a donut, I turned my attention to their siblings who began requesting treats—evidently the same group I had failed to recognize moments earlier.

I offered the remaining donuts to the parents. Thinking that I had successfully fed all interested parties, I gathered up the leftover drinks and last donut and headed for my car. Curiously, I noted one of the mild-mannered moms talking heatedly to the coach. My ears perked up at the hint of potential inequalities. After she left the field I inquired about the conflict. Little did I know what a crushing blow I had inflicted when one sibling did not receive a donut! This oversight was from a mere misunderstanding and not an intentional slight. Why would one child be more deserving over another—the quality of his brother's play? The brother of the offended party happened to be one of the best players on the team.

Being the people-pleasing peacemaker that I am, I immediately went home to confess by e-mail my oversight and innocuous breach of snack duty etiquette. In response to my written apology, I received from the chagrined mom the following e-mail, which she copied to the team:

"Thanks for the sweet after-game snack which turned out to be sour for the siblings. I would think that if the donuts were on sale, they would be cheap enough to pick up another dozen…"

She reminded me of the subtleties of the snack policy, which included bringing sufficient supplies for siblings. Then she concluded by saying:

"Today, what happened was intentionally done which we know is hard to admit. We as parents very well know who the siblings are and if the snacks were not sufficient we as adults could have done without and shared among the siblings. My son *(sibling)* would understand if there were none left, but it was purposefully not offered to him and he felt rejected. Let me tell you my son is a very strong person but he was *inconsolable* because he was rejected. It's not that the kids are greedy; it's the joy of eating together. What happened today should not happen again and let's be there as a team to cheer up our kids!"

I was the one who needed cheering at this point. Let this be a public apology: I never meant to exclude anyone that day. Who knew? Next time I see donuts on sale, I will walk briskly in the opposite direction. I will head straight for the fresh produce aisle and purchase carrot packages for everyone. Then I doubt that players—or their siblings—will be clamoring for more. But first I am going to forget about dieting and eat that last remaining donut.

Bring Your Own Bat—Enduring Child Birthday Bashes

These days kids expect a lot. When did birthday parties become all-day extravaganzas at exotic locations? Growing up, we sat at a table wearing pointed hats awaiting the thrill of blowing out the candles on a homemade cake. That *was* the main event. If we were lucky we played Pin the Tail on the Donkey.

For those who still enjoy the simplicity of a backyard party, the current spin is to bat a bulging piñata—with a blindfold on. It's best not to stand within several feet of the sightless swinger or your wallet will not be the only thing bruised. Be careful that all your private parts and breakables are protected. My friend was left to repair a large crack in her backyard window when one staggering guest strayed off course.

If you don't want to spring for the $12 stash of candy, leftover Halloween candy works too, provided your kids haven't discovered the hiding spot in the attic. Will guests really notice if the chocolate has faded to a dull brown and the gummy worms are now matted into a melted clump of sugar? Isn't the best part lunging after it?

Knowing when to bring out the star attraction is of strategic importance. These days, children are used to being entertained and are easily bored. Thus parties must be crammed with activities and scheduled with military precision.

Such is the approach of my husband, the engineering manager. He expects everything to be carefully choreographed and sandwiched into a one-hour time slot. Left to his control, parties would be held like his work meetings, following a clear agenda and purpose. He always wants to know the plan and to keep the pace moving.

"What's next?" is Sam's mantra—a sharp contrast with the casual affairs where assorted adults lounge about for hours, eating and watching the children frolic.

Take the party for Nico's preschool classmate. Three hours into the party and the cake was finally being served. The presents remained unopened and the star guest of honor—the piñata—remained propped up in the corner. I eyed the door longingly, freedom a mere foot away. My social bunny begged to stay, assuring me that the beating of the piñata was about to begin.

Another half hour passed with no sign of the activity. The paper pirate was sweating bullets in dread of imminent demise.

"Anyone got a stick for the piñata?" an older cousin asked casually. I sensed trouble.

He strolled away in search of a suitable whacking device, returning to the room twenty minutes later carrying a branch. I glanced outside; the tree was missing a limb. Then another relative sauntered off to seek a rope with which to hang the doomed pirate. I wanted to suggest dragging it from the back of my car and letting the children know what block the candy dropped out on.

Instead I bolted for the door, sending Sam along later to retrieve Nico. He brought enough candy home to last until Easter.

At least leaving early spared me the humiliation of watching my present get picked last. I love the parties where they run out of time to open presents, unlike baby showers where opening gifts *is* the main activity. My gift is always the last one chosen. Like the misfit passed over for school games, it languishes conspicuously in the center of the room.

For certain people, gift-wrapping is an art form. Every corner is sealed to perfection. Elaborate bows adorn the box, and ribbons curl down the edges in designs at which even Martha Stewart would marvel. Somehow my box always looks like it was run over by the UPS truck. I pretend my kids wrapped it.

Presents must be elaborate now, so a suitably large swatch of wrapping paper or a gift bag must be found. A puzzle or yo-yo does not cut it; the more batteries required the better. Thankfully, older kids prefer gift cards, eliminating the search for scissors and Scotch Tape. Present value should be comparable to the size of the overstuffed goody bags kids bring home.

I'm not sure what is harder: attending parties or giving them. When hosting a party, one should make it clear if the party is kids-only, or if adults are expected to stay. There are always the parents who drop-and-run and don't look back. During Kyle's sixth birthday Sam and I were left to guard a group of sugar-high first graders careening around a local theme park. Only Sponge Bob the piñata joined us at the picnic table.

For Kyle's fifth birthday we rented the pool of our former condominium for a barbecue, only to discover that the person in charge of the storage room containing the grill forgot to leave us the key. Nothing like a feast of raw meat to bring out the carnivore in all of us!

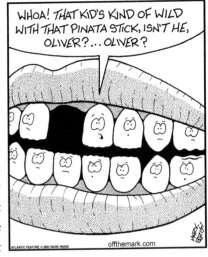

The lack of cooking implements did not alarm me as much as the lack of subtlety from my five-year-old when a heavyset family came to use the pool. Kyle immediately turned to the most obese of the bunch and said in that subtle way only kids can master: "It looks like she had too many donuts."

We like the retro parties held in the backyard, where we have supplies on hand and do not have to worry about guests escaping or uninvited guests arriving. We have matches ready and do not have to resort to rubbing sticks together to ignite the grill or the cake candles. Nor must we run around to random strangers in the park asking, "Do you have a knife?"

It's a good thing we only celebrate our children's birth once a year. Maybe the key is to give birth in a leap year. See you in four years! Just in case, BYOB—Bring Your Own Bat for the *piñata*.

Taking the Plunge—The Extreme Sport of Weddings

If birthday parties have ballooned to new heights of extravagance, weddings involve all the pomp and preparation of a royal coronation. Plans are laid out decades in advance. Families line up key players with the precision of an agent pulling a Super Bowl team together. Day timers are whipped out to establish time lines and game-day strategies. Brides-to-be eagerly pore over dates and browse through bulging books of invitations. Parents secure second mortgages on homes or strategically sell off stock options to pay for it all.

"I do" is in danger of becoming "I'm in debt!"

When I fantasized over marrying my mate, I yanked out a copy of *Farmer's Almanac* from the library shelf to determine what weekend—in three years—we should marry on. (When it later coincided with Sam's final exam, I rescheduled it to the following weekend, rather than sabotage his Masters degree from MIT.)

Off I trotted to the local Kinko's and picked out a modest crème card with burgundy-colored text. A hip, eighty-year-old pastor friend accompanied me to a bridal outlet in Grand Rapids, Michigan. While I perused the sale rack, he made sure I did not pick anything too prudish. Delighted to find a dress my size, I snatched it off the rack and scrubbed out the sweat stains. I wondered if a bride had returned it halfway through the ceremony. Imagine my delight when I discovered across the border a matching pair of bridesmaid dresses on sale for only thirty-six Canadian dollars.

Weddings typically start at a minimum of $20,000, my friend informed me as her daughter announced her engagement. Betrothals must last two years for all the nuptial planning now required. Dinner menus are sampled beforehand and wine lists studiously tested. A hunt for the perfect location begins. The color scheme is decided and the twenty-person bridal party is lined up. A florist and photographer team is secured. By the time the big day arrives tempers are frayed and everyone is careful not to provoke Bridezilla.

When I married Sam in 1984, his father acted as pastor, his brothers joined my twin and childhood friend as the four-person bridal party, and the church ladies doubled as chefs and waitresses. The meal was simple meat-and-potatoes fare. Our reception was held in the church gym—magically transformed into a party room with hanging floral baskets strung from converted basketball hoops. A local nursery provided the plants and bridal arch for a nominal fee. Wedding photos were taken across the street at the boys' reformatory center. The residents there had plenty of free time to beautify the grounds. Conveniently, the motel hosting out-of-town family members was located across the street. Hence relatives could wander over for their turn in front of the camera. This was before cell phones so homing pigeons were sent over to give ample warning.

Post-dinner entertainment consisted of skits, songs, and poems about the bride and groom. There were no band members or bar attendants to pay off. We brought the liquor ourselves and slapped a bottle on each table. The biggest concern was when an important-looking official walked up to the Master of Ceremonies in the middle of the toast. I turned to Sam, "Were we supposed to get a liquor license?" Then we noticed the immigration badge on his shirt. Just as I wondered what crime I had possibly committed by marrying an American, my brother-in-law popped up behind the impersonator with a huge bouquet of balloons. We were not only toasted but roasted!

A few years ago my friend Rachel, my former rafting partner, found an even better bargain on her wedding attire than I did; her slip cost more than the dress did. Like Jesus feeding the five thousand on a few loaves, she managed to host a wedding for two hundred people on two thousand dollars. The sister of the groom presided over the ceremony in a quaint old church. Whoever could not fit inside sat on the steps outdoors. The dinner entertainment was a street musician whom they hired off the street. Payment was determined later based on the quality of his performance. As maid of honor, I helped Rachel shop for the reception dinner ingredients the day before. Items we had mulled over in a distracted fog magically appeared on the buffet table. Family members provided vats of pasta and salads, prepared the previous evening. Barbecue items served by friends consisted of every kind of meat, with sumptuous salads and carb fixes on the side.

The most daunting task of the wedding day was shuttling the bride to the event. Though we are both similarly time-challenged, her family trusted me to find the car keys at the critical moment and reach the church before the prelude. I never saw a happier bride and groom, ecstatic to be together or relieved that I had the keys.

My twin sister wouldn't let a little scare ruin her big day—like her pianist nearly passing out from stomach flu an hour before the service started. With one hand clutching a cell phone, the other flipping through phone books, Hett and I each combed for leads for a replacement. Just as I considered buying a classical music CD for the processional, a fellow patron recruited her piano-playing mother. Not only was she an excellent player, she was willing to drop her plans at a moment's notice. Wedding success does not depend on the amount of money poured into the event; it's about bringing the right people together at the right time.

Then there is the detail of picking the venue. It's not enough for some couples to get hitched in a church or a justice of the peace. That would be too easy (assuming everyone has directions). Couples today tie the knot while bungee jumping, scuba diving, or careening through a log ride. That puts the thrill into "taking the plunge." Others choose a winery, beach, or mountaintop experience. Getting married has become an extreme sport—though some might argue the tougher part is staying married. One wonders, after all the hoopla, how long the typical marriage will last. I read of a couple whose marriage was already being annulled just as the last of the gift checks were clearing the bank.

With all the gift registries couples are signing up for, wedding guests have plenty of stores from which to pick the perfect present. This, however, eliminates the element of surprise. My favorite gift for our dollhouse-sized first apartment was an enormous outdoor thermometer.

No need to sign a pre-nuptial agreement before our marriage; the greatest thing of value was our rusty Toyota that could barely manage to cough up the turnpike. The fewer things we owned, the more fun we had outside. Our most valued possessions could be crammed into the back of our two-door hatchback. With our budget wedding, we did not start our marriage in the red or force our parents to postpone their retirement.

Who knows what grand event we will throw after we've been married thirty or fifty years? We may be ready to push each other off a plane by then. Perhaps we can renew our vows on the way down! I'm sure I can find a skydiving pastor on the Internet.

No Way Out—Navigating the Consumer Maze

Since the key to marital harmony is a good night's sleep, I decided it was high time to replace our mattress. It had an annoying habit of rolling us to an abyss in the center of the bed. At least this was an improvement over the early part of our marriage, when a secondhand bed frame sent us crashing to the floor, or we woke up in a pool of water after the waterbed burst.

When IKEA opened a store in Silicon Valley, I set off to explore the latest fashions in the bedding world. Optimistic, I followed the stream of cars towards the large blue and yellow sign. First, there was the effort to find the optimal parking spot near the entrance. Then there was the flood of impulse items that beckoned. (Stores are deliberately designed to overwhelm us into buying what we probably don't need in the first place. Spend more to save more.)

I curved around a spiral of concrete. After parking and walking for a mile, I found the front entrance to the store. This built endurance for what was soon to come. I merged with other bodies, moving up the escalators toward the double sliding doors and $199-couch display.

The key to mastering IKEA, I learned, is to be wary of the Exit sign. It is a one-way trap from which you cannot escape. No windows and glass doors serve as reference points, just the circuitous arrow that finally culminates at the cash registers.

Following the gray arrow toward the bedroom section, my eyes glazed over at this orgy of domesticity. A plethora of choices greeted me. In the latex Sultan line, there was the Egersund, Enebakk, Erfjord, and Evje. In the foam line there was the Forsen, Fangebo, Fageras, and Forsbacka. I preferred a mattress with a pronounceable name and traditional springs and coils. The frames were no more promising; the prospect of searching for a matching boxed set to stuff into the car and assemble at home was too frightening. A crucial component would inevitably be missing and I would have to return. I opted to bail, ignoring the arrow. If all else failed I would follow the smells of Swedish meatballs and salmon towards the cafeteria.

Just when I wondered if I would ever see my family again, I spied the escalator that had propelled me from the parking lot. It dumped shoppers into the store, but it did not return them to their cars. Sneaking through an employee door, I discovered natural light again and the street ramp. I aimed my car towards the nearest Mattress Discounters store.

Upon my arrival, a salesman immediately pounced, touting the latest one-day-only sale event of the year. The varying amounts of coils and gauges all promised different degrees of comfort and a better night's rest. There was looser stitching and tighter stitching, for a bouncy feel or a dense feel (like stepping into a Volvo). Now shoppers have to become sewing connoisseurs too. That was just the beginning.

The salesman then steered me over to the Ferrari of the bedding world, where he lectured me about the countless varieties of foam, such as memory, breathable, isotonic, and visco-elastic. With each new layer of foam, the mattress grows fatter—until a stepladder is required to climb into it.

Beds are no longer called mattresses—they are sleeping systems. Some systems tout special technology from Sweden; others boast NASA-patented technology designed for astronauts to withstand G-forces. I don't know who needs to withstand that kind of serious motion in bed, but I do know I've been married too long for that. (If you're not generating enough heat in bed, the Tempur-Pedic models tend to run warm as they insulate and hold in body temperature.) There were posturepedic, osteopedic, and tempurpedic beds. Next were the adjustable mattresses, air mattresses, and zoned mattresses with numbered sleeping zones corresponding to various body parts.

By this time I was beginning to zone out myself. If all the choices didn't make my head spin, the prices did. For the $3,500 price tags displayed on the higher-end models, I half expected them to drive off on wheels. I spent less on my first car.

To further confuse the consumer, no two mattresses are called by the same name, so it is impossible to compare prices. The salesman stated, "Each store uses their own names to give mattresses personality." No wonder mattresses cost so much—they not only breathe, they have personalities as well.

"The consumer is making it more difficult than it needs to be," he added, while he could barely keep his own product line straight. He implored me to keep it simple by settling on the desired features and then narrowing it down to a few finalists. This he said while standing in front of no less than six Sealy "systems," all of which offered roughly the same feel and the same price. If only I could choose between the Luxury Firm or the Semi Plush, or the Pillowtop.

The salesman offered to lie down next to me to demonstrate the amazing motionless coil system of the Simmons Beautyrest.

"You won't even notice that your partner is in the same bed," he promised. Right as he snuggled up next to me to prove his point, his wife walked up for a lunch date.

We hadn't even gotten to the pillows yet. They came in Egyptian cotton, hypo-allergenic, and mildew-resistant choices for droolers. Some pillows allegedly cured sleep problems and snoring for those wanting to cure two problems at once. The salesman suggested I jump on the memory foam pillow at home for fifty minutes to soften it up. If I really wanted a workout, I would go to the gym.

Then there were the mattress covers and mattress toppers, specially designed to protect these costly investments from the layers of sweat that we exude over time, and the nine pounds of skin that we shed each year. Each "sleeping system" came with a "hassle-free comfort exchange." Undoubtedly it would be more painful to return the mattress than to keep it. No mention was made of the extra delivery charges and no warning given that we might not find the same kind of "deal" again. The only comparable price to the one first quoted was the "guest room model." (This is where you put the low-end mattress for visitors in hopes of keeping their visit brief.) I was encouraged to "break the mattress in" for four to eight weeks.

"Try jumping on it for a while," he advised, "to speed up the process."

Here we go again with the jumping.

After this spree I was ready to shop for something safe and simple, like shampoo. I trotted off to the local grocery store.

There, more choices awaited me: shampoo for dry hair, greasy hair, normal hair, "rebellious" hair, frizzy hair, chemically challenged hair.... I counted ten different varieties of one brand alone. What must foreign-born folks think about shopping in America? It's no wonder we are a nation with sleep problems; life today offers more choices than we know what to do with.

All these choices had me worn out and ready for bed. If I could just decide which herbal tea to sip: chamomile or peppermint; which of two hundred channels to watch; which toothbrush to use: ultrasonic firm or regular soft; which toothpaste: extra fluoride or ultra white?

Now to settle on whether to keep my new mattress—I'll sleep on that.

All I Don't Need for Christmas—Avoiding Holiday Hoopla

Every year our local Christmas in the Park in San Jose, California is transformed into a more ambitious affair. What began as a modest showing of a few decorative storefronts has evolved into an increasingly elaborate display of lights, traveling carnival rides, singing teddy bear Santas, and a food court.

Christmas decorations have taken on a life of their own, as have Halloween displays. Perhaps we should combine the two in a marriage of orange and white lights, since stores now start selling holiday items by summer. How soon to start shopping and shipping? Can we enjoy the season just as much without the flurry of activities?

In December 1984, I was spared the guilt of shipping gifts after Christmas to avoid postal lines. That was the only occasion where I persuaded Sam to brave holiday traffic and snowstorms to visit my family in Canada. When his beard transformed into a frozen waterfall one blustery evening, he abandoned for good the notion of spending Christmas anywhere but California. He would just as soon avoid crowds and weather delays and not spend Christmas Day stranded in a Midwest airport terminal.

Each balmy November the boys begin begging, "When can we put up the lights?" This is followed closely by, "When can we put the tree together?" We opt against snatching a discarded tree from the curb the day after Christmas and haul down from the attic our three-piece tree with attached lights. This eliminates debates about portly trees versus slim trees and Douglas fir over Noble pine. (Inevitably husbands and wives have grown up in opposite camps.) After the tree is assembled and decorated the kids immediately ask, "When can we put presents under the tree?"

"Can we open just *one* present?"

"Hey, how come he has more?"

One thing leads to another until only a single box remains unopened on Christmas morning.

Each year we face the big decisions over opening presents on Christmas Eve versus Christmas Day and whether to stay at home or go elsewhere.

Once we drove six hours to visit Sam's side of the family. Eying the bulging packages beautifully wrapped under the tree, we panicked over the paltry items we had purchased for them the week before. Excusing ourselves, we dashed off to upgrade our supply, in search of a store still open on Christmas Eve.

"Would a box of See's chocolates sweeten the deal?" I asked Sam in a hurried tone.

"Who needs the extra calories during the holidays?"

"Perhaps another set of calming candles. You can't go wrong with candles, even if these are too pretty to light up."

We grabbed our finds and rushed back for dinner. If only we had started shopping months earlier. Of course, then we would have been unable to locate our hidden stash when needed. Fearing failure, we typically cave into doubt and purchase a back-up gift on Christmas Eve.

Spotting a two-for-one sale, we select a second sweater for a sibling to even the score.

We promise ourselves to scale back next year.

Our family began that next Christmas season by donating money toward items that impoverished people need most. These are not backscratchers and foot massagers, but soybeans, medicines, water filters, and tree seedlings, to name a few. In lieu of JC Penney and Target holiday ads, we browsed through relief agency wish lists.

"PEACE ON EARTH" is my new mantra, not "Let there be a parking spot left at the mall." In fretting over all the festivities of Christmas, it's easy to forget the true spirit of the season. While considering life's abundant blessings, let's vow to share our time and wealth with others at this holy season and throughout the remaining eleven months of the year.

My life, like yours, does not always resemble the cozy fireplace mantle scenes from Hallmark commercials. What I lack in innate ability, I make up for in effort, as I strive to maintain balance and perspective. Regardless of what battles befall me, or the world, I resolve to spread light and encouragement to people around me. With an abiding faith, a respect for my fellow men, and the love of family and friends cheering from the sidelines… what could go wrong?

About the Author

Yvonne Linton has written for local newspapers, magazines, and nonprofit newsletters. Though she is a past winner of the Toasmasters' Tall Tales Contest, no stories in this book have been changed to protect the guilty. Some names have been changed to protect the innocent.

Since her sleep issues have greatly improved, she admits her life contains far less drama. Thankfully, it is never dull. After a successful career in textbook publishing, Yvonne has returned to the education field as a substitute teacher. Here, adapting on the fly serves her well.

Now that her twin has relocated to the West coast, Yvonne looks forward to sharing more escapades in years to come.

A Canadian transplant to the San Francisco Bay Area, she has been married to Sam for twenty-five years. They have two sons, Kyle and Nico, and a menagerie of pets.

www.yvonnelinton.com